CLOUDLANDS MEMOIRS

STORIES OF CONTEMPORARY PAPUA NEW GUINEA

Published by Brolga Publishing Pty Ltd
ABN 46 063 962 443
PO BOX 12544, A'Beckett Street,
Melbourne, Victoria, Australia, 8006

email: bepublished@brolgapublishing.com.au
web: www.brolgapublishing.com.au

National Library of Australia
Cataloguing-in-Publication entry

Le Fevre, Laurie
Cloudlands Memoirs
ISBN- 10 1920785868
ISBN- 13 9781920785866

1. Le Fevre, Laurie. 2. Australians - Papua New Guinea - Biography. I. Title.

995.30092

Printed in Singapore
Cover Design by David Khan
Typeset by Yeni Cahyadi

CLOUDLANDS MEMOIRS

by

Laurie Le Fevre

Happy birthday
Sue —

all good wishes.

Laurie Le Fevre

24 Oct 2006

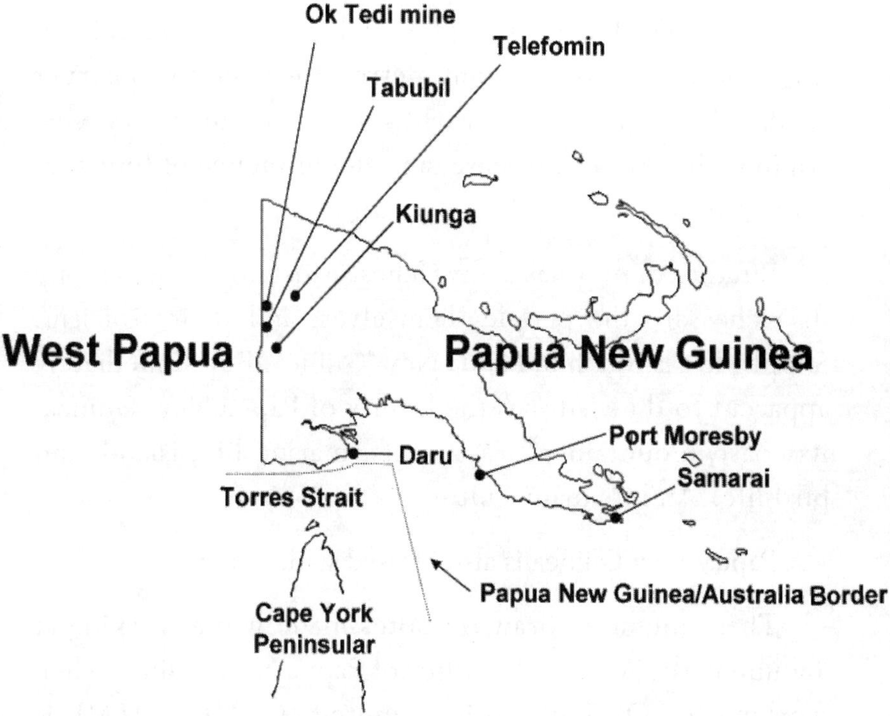
Ok Tedi mine
Telefomin
Tabubil
Kiunga
West Papua
Papua New Guinea
Port Moresby
Daru
Samarai
Torres Strait
Papua New Guinea/Australia Border
Cape York
Peninsular

FOREWORD

God chose special people to populate Papua New Guinea. People of lesser stuff would not have coped with the enormous challenges the country has for its people.

Challenges like growing food where the annual rainfall might be a soil-eroding eight metres, the need to construct roads within one of the world's great mountain systems, coping with tropical disease, and the influence of four tectonic plates.

But the country has many riches. Most important among its riches are the people themselves, and their stoicism. Simply, life is tough in Papua New Guinea. But immediately apparent to the visitor is the beauty of Papua New Guinea: its coast, mountains, forest, reefs, marine life, island, and bird life. And its many cultures.

Papua New Guinea is also blessed with minerals.

These memoirs draw on notes made while working at Tabubil in the Western Province of Papua New Guinea when working for Ok Tedi Mining Limited (OTML). OTML is located at one of the worlds most remote mine sites – the Star Mountains of Papua New Guinea, or the "Cloudlands". OTML produces copper and gold. The logistical effort required supporting successful mining and processing in such a location is of a huge scale that is almost beyond imagination.

But the people of Papua New Guinea, who make up 95% of the workforce at OTML, are very special and rise to the challenges. OTML is justified in adopting the well-worn claim of its workforce being its greatest asset.

These stories serve today to remind me of the people with whom I worked at OTML, of their abilities, their application, their sense of humour, and their friendship. They also attempt to make a positive statement about contemporary Papua New Guinea. The press coverage of Papua New Guinea is largely limited to the bad news. Certainly such news events should be reported, but some balance is needed. Australia shares an international border with Papua New Guinea, and the Australian High Commission in Port Moresby is reported now to be Australia's largest overseas post. Australia needs to know more about its nearest neighbour, and to show more neighbourly understanding and generosity, even if only for reasons of self-interest. Papua New Guinea on the other hand shares international borders with two other countries – Solomon Islands and the West Papua Province of Indonesia. It is easy for Australia as an island state to forget its important place in the Pacific, that it has such close international connections, and that it has a stabilising effect in a potentially unstable region.

The stories are not just about people, but they meander in and out of themes particular people suggest. These people are remarkable for their achievements; some have moved on to other organisations; some have retired. Sadly, one died tragically, but she lives on in our memories. But the essential message does not change - these are special people.

CONTENTS

The Invitation Back

Pat and I had been two of the thousands of Australians who worked in Papua New Guinea in the pre-independence era.

We met in our twenties on the beautiful island of Samarai in the Milne Bay Province. We married in Port Moresby, and over many years lived and worked in what today are the Western Highlands, Chimbu, National Capital District and Milne Bay provinces.

We eventually left Papua New Guinea in 1971 after ten years there.

Over several years Pat, a nurse, and ever adaptable, had practiced her profession in general nursing, midwifery and infant welfare, from the coast to the highlands, in major hospitals and village aid posts.

I worked in several government departments, the greater part of the time being spent in the central coordinating agency, the (then) Department of the Administrator. This included a period of three years in the 1960s looking after the welfare of Indonesian political refugees.

Our first house after we were married was built of bamboo and thatch. Designed for earthquake conditions, the house sat on four huge beams that spanned the four rocks that were the corners of a square. I often wondered how they were moved to site. It was a quiet house as the thatch muffled the sound of the rain, but the house and earth regularly moved as the tectonic plates stirred. Some of the earthquakes resulted in considerable damage to the town, but no-one seemed terribly concerned.

Later on, after our son Andrew had arrived, we moved into a house of another vernacular – the Australian-derived fibro-cement sheet house that now widely infects Papua New Guinea. Noisy when it rained, its only redeeming feature was and is there is no need for a python in the ceiling to keep the rat population down (it's a fallacy, but it made for great conversation).

Between us we experienced many of the adventures Papua New Guinea provides. Pat got to the Trobriand Islands (I missed out but am still working on it!), we climbed 4,000 metre mountains, sailed and snorkeled in Milne Bay, walked or motor-cycled the tracks of the Chimbu, and four-wheel drove the Highlands Highway when a 4wd was a tool, rather than a suburban aspiration.

We acquired reasonable skills in Tok Pisin and Hiri Motu, which along with English make up the three official languages of Papua New Guinea. There are 700 more languages in Papua New Guinea, and we probably had exposure to only two or three of them. Sometimes this resulted in simply learning some basic words of greeting; in another case Pat had to acquire enough Melpa, the Mount Hagen language, to practice her craft with the Mount Hagen mothers.

We learnt to live with *dahori* ("later" in Motu – like mañana in Spanish, but lacking the associated sense of urgency), and we learnt that *dimdim* was not an insult, but the Milne Bay word for the Caucasians.

But it was all over in 1971 when we eventually re-established ourselves in Australia, re-established careers, and had a beautiful daughter, Madeleine. Madeleine has not as yet visited Papua New Guinea, but has a Papuan godmother whom she adores. And when Maddy married her Roberto our Papua New Guinea friends sent them traditional weddings gifts – a woman's food bag for her, and bone tipped arrows for him. That Madeleine has not yet visited Papua New Guinea is but a technicality to the Papua New Guineans, who chose to send wedding presents to their friends.

Maybe this indicates there is no use by date on friendship. In a Papua New Guinean woman's reflections on friendship in her poem This is My Day, Margaret Dull, a flight attendant with OTML's airline says "…Friends are for ever, and friends do not say never…"

The Papua New Guinea connection persisted and we maintained an involvement with several Papua New Guinea networks. In my Australian government roles anything that smacked of Papua New Guinea seemed to be hand-balled to me, and I undertook many tasks for the Papua New Guinea government from afar.

Job offers were made too – usually by visiting Papua New Guinea bureaucrats who wanted me back in country. A cruise in 1999 provided the perfect opportunity to revisit old haunts, so find our old house on Samarai, to see the remains of one of Pat's old hospitals, to visit the war sites in East and West New Britain and Milne Bay, and for Pat to get to practice her now little used Tok Pisin with a group of mothers and children at the Madang market. She could not help herself; a group of mothers and babies in any society always triggers the urge to go and talk with them.

Shortly after the cruise a serendipitous event occurred. It was a phone call from a colleague in a major Australian corporation, one of those phone calls that start with "You might be interested in something we are doing…"

He referred to the Ok Tedi mine site in Papua New Guinea. Would I be interested?

What could I say?

Setting the Scene

David Danga stopped me in Dakon Road one day to ask if I had ever worked in the Chimbu Province.

Yes, I had.

David remembered me from earlier times when he was a schoolboy. I looked at his name on his shirt and asked if he were Danga Mondo's son.

Yes, he is.

I worked with Danga Mondo in the past when he was a director of Chimbu Coffee Limited, which at the time was the largest Papua New Guinean-owned enterprise, with around 10,000 Chimbu shareholders.

After that road-side meeting David and I spoke often. He looked forward to seeing the photos of the old Chimbu days when l brought them back from leave, running his fingers over the images of the people he knew as a child as though he were reading Braille.

Old Danga eventually sent through David a request for some current photos of friends from the old days. We sent photos through to Danga – a group of his old friends in a state of formality that Danga had never seen us – lounge suits for a wedding. From all accounts, Danga was suitably impressed.

On the same road a few days later another young man ran to catch up with me, hand extended for a Hagen handshake – one up; one down. He greeted me in the Hagen language, Melpa. "*Kabuga*?" (all OK?) he enquired. "*Kabuga morum*" (pretty good) I replied, exhausting my knowledge of Melpa in the one exchange.

"I'm just back from Mount Hagen" he explained, catching his breath. "My grandfather said he used to know you".

It was Nicholas Wamp, grandson of Sir Wamp Wan. Before he went out on his field break we had had a conversation about Mount Hagen. I had enquired about Sir Wamp's health.

Sir Wamp Wan, the great Mount Hagen leader, became the face of Mount Hagen following the death in 1963 of another great leader, Ninji. Wamp was an accomplished orator in the Highlands tradition, and I recall the occasion when he declared his vision for Papua New Guinea of the future in Tok Pisin as "New Guinea Papua and Australia as one."

Many highlanders used the form "New Guinea Papua". He demonstrated his meaning by clasping his hands together tightly, making the point to the assembled crowd. Nick Wamp, his grandson, today works for OTML.

We knew Sir Wamp well in the past. A generation ago, on a Saturday visit to Mount Hagen from Kerowagi, Pat, Andrew and I were at the market where we ran into Wamp. Wamp was pleased to see us after an absence of three years, and immediately took to Andrew.

So delighted was Wamp with Andrew that he took him on horseback to the village of Rebiamaul on the outskirts of the town to show the women, proudly returning with him later in the day.

***

It was always a warm experience making connections such as these.

I admit to the desire I share with most people who have an earlier association with Papua New Guinea to relive the earlier times, and seek connections. Maybe it is to validate the experiences, the stories of which tend to receive more embellishment the more distant the occurrence.

And many books have been written about earlier times, especially books of the pre-independence era. Generally these are excellent pieces of first person memory rather than works of history. But fact is an interpretative condition when viewed from a distance, and history gives way to reminiscing.

But I wonder if Danga and Wamp really remembered me. Like most of us maybe they remembered what they thought they remembered from the days when New Guinea Papua and Australia really did ***pas wantaim***.

***

Karonama Ani met me at the Tabubil Airport. We touched palms through the mesh security fence and started chatting even before Customs and Migration formalities were sorted out. We had met a few months earlier when Karonama was appointed to the role of Contracts Supervisor at OTML. I was engaged to work as his mentor, and we became good friends over the following months.

Karonama Ani is an architect and registered builder by

profession. He was born on the South Papuan coast, undertook his high schooling at Aiyura High School and later earned his degree at Unitech Lae. We shared an interest in how the new and the traditional sometimes conflict, and often used the example of the disappearance of the traditional South Papuan coast architecture, and its substitution with the epidemic of cement sheet clad houses that now stretches from Port Moresby eastwards to Hood Lagoon.

The traditional houses had a majesty that will never be seen again. They were a stunning sight from the water, with soaring three-dimensional gables that approached Gothic in their visual impact and shared (and probably predated) similar structural principles to the Gothic arch. Form followed function, and the houses had beautiful living qualities, including views to the sea. And importantly the materials did not have to be imported. Karonama often discussed with me the principle of form following function in relation to the design of business systems. It was a useful analogy.

Sadly, Karonama had not seen the traditional houses of the culture of which he is part. Later however I was able to give him photos taken years before he was born.

Wonderful storeys.

Karonama's wife Olive, and their beautiful daughters of primary school age, Leilani and Ilawendy, also became friends, and I transitioned into being *Bubu* (grandpa). Karonama and Olive's wish for a third daughter was realised later, and today they are the proud parents of another daughter, a pre-schooler,

Iamolua.

Karonama Ani's route into his contracting role was from architecture into building contracting and management in a number of government agencies. Architecture remains one of his first loves. The other is his family. Today he has an executive position in the resources sector in Australia.

***

Life is full of coincidences. The first of the OTML connections with the past occurred on that first flight on the company Dash 8 flight from Cairns to Tabubil.

One of the flight attendants looked familiar. I recognised her as a Miss Papua New Guinea entrant from the time of our earlier cruise to Papua New Guinea, but the tentative and self-conscious smile of the publicity shots then had given way to today's self confidence.

Some months later, when I was working on the site, Delores told me she was born Delores Ling. Delores is the daughter of Clare Ling who was the first Papua New Guinea woman to be accredited as a flight attendant on the Dash 8 that Delores now flew. I recalled that Jim Sinclair had written about Clare in his monumental book about aviation in Papua New Guinea, Balus.

I had never met Clare, but Delores told me her story. Clare is from Bipi Island in Manus Province. Bipi Island is known among other things for its dancing. The daughter of a schoolteacher, Clare had been taught from an early age the value of education. She trained and graduated as a nurse at Vunapope in East New Britain and worked as a nurse in various hospitals. Clare met George Ling in 1976 when she moved to New Ireland to work at the Kavieng General Hospital.

Delores would be their only daughter, as George died in 1982.

In the meantime Clare had swapped her nurse's uniform for that of a flight attendant with Air Niugini. She flew every aircraft in the fleet, but took time off to again pursue her nursing career. However flying attracted her back again and Clare resumed flying - this time with Talair, where she became chief flight attendant. It seemed from Delores' account that Clare had become addicted to uniforms but could not decide which one she preferred. In any event her appointment as chief flight attendant was another significant step in the advancement of Papua New Guineans.

In 1987 she re-married. Her new husband, Henry Chow Jr, became Delores' father. Delores' love for Henry was demonstrated when she adopted his name.

Today Clare and Henry have two other children – Alyssa and Michael. Clare insisted on Alyssa completing her high schooling in Brisbane. Michael will also move to Brisbane when he is of high school age.

Clare and Henry have a number of business interests in Papua New Guinea including retail stores and hair dressing salons. Delores, a snip off the old lock, has also worked as a hairdresser and in business, and also had some of her education in Brisbane.

I got to know Delores well, and she paid me the compliment of treating me like a favourite uncle in an extended family – Melanesian style.

***

A flick through the OTML phone directory revealed many names that connect with the past. From Amion to Zurenuoc there are more than enough apparent threads to weave a carpet of connections.

It is inevitable I suppose. OTML is one of Papua New Guinea's leading corporations. OTML is one of the largest corporate contributors to the Papua New Guinea economy. It maintains this position not just through the good fortune of a treasure trove of copper and gold, and an insatiable market, but also through management leadership and rigour. In the pursuit of self interest, OTML recruits the best of the Papua New Guinea graduates, pays the best wages in Papua New Guinea, treats its staff well, provides the best learning opportunities and support, and operates what is arguably the best public hospital in Papua New Guinea today. As a consequence, it retains the best quality people, although the resources boom in Australia has been responsible for some selective recruitment of Papua New Guinea professionals from OTML.

Whilst it is fashionable for organisations today to mouth platitudinous that its staff are its greatest asset, OTML simply demonstrates its attitude towards its employees and the people of the Western Province and the Star Mountains.

Not surprisingly therefore, the best people gravitate to OTML and its satellite partners.

"Look at the names," I thought. "Look at the connections with the past".

David Siwi works for Starwest Constructions. He is the son of Siwi Kurondo who was elected to the House of Assembly in 1964 and later became Under-Secretary for Forests. David's sister Dorothy was married in Mt Hagen in the 60s in a ceremony that I attended.

Later in Kerowagi in 1969, I had to undertake a census of coffee plantings. Siwi Kurondo's assistance ensured the success of the project. In this area of Papua New Guinea counting was undertaken on a base two. This was not binary, but a method of counting that went along the lines of one, two, two plus one, two plus two, etc.

Whilst it met most needs it was not conducive to dealing with the numbers with which we would be working. Siwi Kurondo's strategy was that plantation owners would pluck a twig from each of their trees and bring them to me in bundles for counting.

Siwi himself had several acres under coffee, and probably 1000 coffee trees as I recall. Coffee was a successful cash crop.

Today it is joined by cardamom as the more successful cash crops in the Kerowagi Sub-Province.

At the time Siwi was Under-Secretary for Forests, and he often took me into his confidence about his particular interest in the coffee industry. "It grows on trees" he would explain. This was not false logic; it was just a provocative political point he liked to make.

***

And the names Anna and Robert Papa. I had to ask if there was a connection with Robin Papat. Yes, there is. Robert is the son of Robin Papat who was one of the first Papua New Guinea journalists to work for the Australian Broadcasting Commission, which he had joined as a cadet.

Robert is an Instrument Technician by trade, but now works in the Procurement Team. Anna has a black belt – not in judo but in the Operating Excellence methodology, Six Sigma.

Robin Papat is from Matupit Island in Rabaul. As a cadet, he trained with the Australian Broadcasting Commission in Australia, and became a broadcaster in Canberra. Back in Papua New Guinea his career in broadcasting was almost solely in Rabaul, where he employed his skills as a journalist, translator, tape-splicer, and broadcaster in English, Kuanua (one of East New Britain languages) and Tok Pisin as the occasion needed. Multi-skilling was expected of the Papua New Guinea broadcasters before the term was coined.

Broadcasting in East New Britain in the mid-1960s to mid-70s had some challenges. There was the potential for political interference, when the highly divisive, but democratically elected, Gazelle multi-racial council was established. The Mataungan Association, a Tolai political body, challenged the election of the Council, and then to further confuse the matter a group of expatriate Tolais in Port Moresby formed the Warmaran group and sought to intervene. This group, named after the Kuanua word for mediation, had strong support from government, but the ABC, true to its charter, only broadcast the facts.

None the less it was a period of instability, and Robin Papat's voice stood out in troubled times as the voice of reason. Listening to him reading the news was one of the delights of the lunch hour in those years.

Today he is retired from broadcasting, and manages Anna and Robert's cocoa plantation at Warangoi.

Anna graduated from the Goroka Business College in 1988 as a Stenographer and almost immediately joined OTML. Anna followed the route of many other such OTML recruits in that she was soon promoted to higher levels, firstly the administrative ranks, then recruitment, and more recently into the Operating Excellence program.

Along the way she completed a Diploma of Human Resource Management at the Divine Word University at Madang through distance learning. Anna, wife, mother of three, and a full time employee, is now looking for further challenges.

And the black belt? This was awarded following four months of the highly specific training required to certify for a Six Sigma Black Belt. This was largely undertaken at conferences and workshops in Australia where she Anna also developed skills as an ambassador for her country.

***

I guessed from the name that Finkewe Zurenuoc was the daughter of Zure Makili Zurecnuoc, who I had known when he was Under-Secretary for the Treasury.

When the opportunity to meet Finkewe Zurenuoc arose I asked, not that I needed to as I saw the undeniable family resemblance immediately. Yes, notwithstanding the minor difference in the spelling of their names, Finkewe's father is Zure Zurecnuoc. Originally a schoolteacher he later pursued a political career. Again, I was able to produce a photo of her father from those days.

The Zurecnuoc family features widely in Papua New Guinea history as soldiers, government officials, teachers, and medical assistants.

Whatever was passed on to the next generation was obviously beneficial as Finkewe Zurenuoc is one of Papua New Guinea's most highly regarded engineers.

***

The Kerowagi High School magazine of 1970 reported

that Mary Gena, as she was then known, was in 2A that year. The brief pen picture of Mary (as contributed by her peers) was "a clever girl who tells funny stories".

Dr Miila Gena is now a physician in the Western Province after a career that has gone full circle. Dr Gena made a name for herself as a physician, then as a health administrator, and later became the Secretary of what then was the Department of Home Affairs.

She later came to Ok Tedi as a doctor, earning a level of respect from the people that approached reverence. The Papua New Guinea public health system in the Western Province is a cot case itself, so Dr Gena soon shifted her attention from healing patients to healing the system – with substantial support and help from OTML – much to its credit. She came up with strategies of which a Secretary of a department would be proud, and immersed herself in the physical work involved in the actual construction of facilities.

I ran into Dr Gena at the airport one morning. She was wearing her khaki uniform, safety boots and yellow safety helmet for the short flight back to Kiunga where she was supervising a construction job. The queue and the milling crowd notwithstanding, her greeting was Chimbu-style, her arm around me and her head on my arm.

I remember Miila when she was called Mary as very serious, gifted, and destined for great things. And, yes, she did tell funny stories, quietly though.

***

When I was making travel arrangements for a leave break I spoke with the travel clerk, Sussan Songoa. Sussan and her husband Kaia are veterans of many years in the mining industry in Papua New Guinea, working at both Ok Tedi and Porgera.

In the course of the completion of forms we discussed our homes. Sussan knows Australia well, so Melbourne was not a problem.

But she challenged me with "You won't know my place."

"Try me", I said

"Chimbu Province. Do you know it?"

"Yes I do, but where?"

"Kerowagi Sub-Province. Do you know it?"

"Yes I do, but where?"

"You can't possibly know my village."

"Try me".

"Gagl"

"Gagl? I know it well".

More correctly, I once knew Gagl well. I had worked in Kerowagi for two years and visited Gagl regularly. It is a beautiful highland village, to the northeast of Kerowagi, about 15 minutes away by motorcycle across a gentle valley that rises to the ridge where Gagl is located. At the centre of Gagl were a school and a small sports field. Like most playing fields it was definitely not level. In fact it was built on a significant slope.

I brought back photos of Gagl to show Sussan. Almost inevitably she found a picture of an uncle.

"Do you know he died?" she asked, pointing to his photo.

Indeed I did. He died of cancer when we were there.

He was at best guess middle-aged when we knew him. He spoke no English and only a few words of Tok Pisin. We spoke only a few words of Kuman, but each week he brought fresh fruit to our house to sell. It was fruit from his garden at Gagl.

What the magic of Gagl was we never discovered. What special alchemy produced our bananas of preference, the most fragrant of pawpaws, and the sweetest of pineapples, I did not learn. Was it the water that percolated through the limestone, or the orientation, or maybe the old man's special touch?

The Baliem Valley in West Papua is often referred to as Shangri La, but there are a thousand valleys in the highlands of Papua New Guinea that have their own special beauty too. Visiting them was a privilege we took for granted.

Sussan Songoa is Gena of the Silkukane clan. However she spent many years away from home as her father, Onguglo Wena, worked for Correctional Services in other parts of Papua New Guinea. Sussan rebuilt her connections by returning home to do grades 4, 5 and 6 at the Gagl Community School.

The Gena people today are subject to ongoing land pressures through a continuing dispute with the Siklu people. It is a claim for land that has been going on for decades, if not longer.

Sussan's husband Kaia is from the Biangai tribe of Wau. Because of the land pressure at Gagl she rarely visits her own home now, and formally resides at Wau. It is a most basic need of the human being to have a sense of belonging, and I try to understand how Sussan feels when she describes her feeling of dislocation.

Language

The death of the Divine Word Missionary, Father Frank Mihalic, occurred soon after my arrival at Tabubil. Father Frank Mihalic who did so much to record and promote Tok Pisin, had produced one of the definitive Tok Pisin grammars and dictionaries. A newspaper cartoon published the week after his death, recognising his contribution to Papua New Guinea, saw Father Mihalic remonstrating with a Papua New Guinean for not speaking pure pidgin. This was an appropriate gesture to a fine man who had spent the majority of his life in Papua New Guinea.

At the time of its independence in 1975 the Independent State of Papua New Guinea chose to have three official languages, of which one would be English.

Maybe this reflected wisdom. Maybe it was pragmatism. In any event to choose the common language of commerce as an official language has given the country a distinct advantage. It is the language of many of its trading partners. It is the principal language of the British Commonwealth - the language that binds. It is the language that embodies so much of the history and the culture of the parliamentary, judicial and legal systems the country has adopted.

And I read recently that Finland is now planning to formally adopt English as its second language so that it better competes in its markets and in the European community. It is very smart and pragmatic of the Fins to dismantle one of the fences between them and their markets. But the Fins always were pragmatic in matters relating to language. Their language uses phonetic spelling, that is, there is only one sound for each letter, and each word has only one pronunciation. This is the case too with the Papua New Guinea languages.

Just as Papua New Guinea chose English as one of its official languages, it also chose Hiri Motu, the trading language that evolved over centuries by the people of Central Province and the people of the Gulf Province. Its adoption was as deeply symbolic as the hiri itself. It is still a major cultural and trading activity. It is a micro representation of the broader trading in which Papua New Guinea engages today.

Then there was Tok Pisin. The Melanesian pidgin language. Curiously, although "pidgin" was the spelling used over many years, I do believe it was the only word in Tok Pisin to use a soft "g". But I am happy to be corrected.

Tok Pisin is the patois of the people. Its vocabulary draws on English (most of the vocabulary in absolute terms), Papua New Guinea languages, German, Portuguese, Indonesian, Latin, but not Finnish I dare say, although there are probably origins in other languages the philologists will eventually get to as they continue to study the origins of its words. However its grammar is distinctly Melanesian.

I found that an indication of a foreigner's imminent departure from OTML can be an interest in learning some Tok Pisin. "Give us a few words will you," I am asked. No doubt they will be used to enliven dinner parties at home, but the interest also reflects a major change at OTML, in that there is almost no need today for Tok Pisin. Until recently Tok Pisin classes for foreigners were provided by OTML, but the need has evaporated. It is a pity in a sense, as language carries with it the code to the culture.

A random selection of some Tok Pisin words can be used to illustrate the broad origins of its vocabulary –

abus	Meat, or condiment – probably a Kuanua word
ananas	Pineapple. From the German. It is a widely used word in Eastern and Western Europe, but not Spain. Ananas had almost disappeared from use by the 1960s, and replaced by painap, but has appeared again in the Tok Pisin I hear being used by the West Papuan refugees, so may be part of the Dutch connection.
arere	edge – possibly from the English arriss, or the French arête (edge)
bagarup	damaged; broken. From the English bankrupt. Adopted in the 1930s when many businesses came and went (bankrupt) during the gold boom.
gumi	anything rubber. Origins are considered to be uncertain, but could range from the English gum, to the Greek komi (rubber), or any number of other European languages. It formerly meant anything from a condom to a

motor tyre, but condom today is often called karamap. (This causes some confusion as karamap is also a packaged lunch.)

kanai seagull – probably Kuanua

kulau green coconut – Kuanua

lewa love; a widely-used, non-intimate, greeting. It is a little like a mother-in-law's dear.
The origin is probably German (liebe).

lotu church – Fijian

mangi small boy – generally accepted as having its origins in English (monkey or mannequin). The form manki is not used today, and will cause offence if used.

maski don't worry; ignore it. Probably from the German es macht nichts, but there is a school of thought that says it could have a Chinese origin.

nasuwi eggplant – Kuanua

Paska Easter – from the Latin pascal

pato duck – Portuguese

pren	lover – from the English friend. Can also mean friend, but be careful with pren as it suggests a connection that may not exist in reality. To be on the safe side, use poro instead if the friendship is platonic.
raus	remove, or chase away – a German word
susu	milk or breast – Indonesian in origin

Three official languages. To many Papua New Guineans it can be an oddity that a country as large as Australia has but one official language. "How do you cope with just one language?" I am asked; "Isn't it limiting?" asks Karonama Ani.

The three official languages aside, Papua New Guinea has many other languages, some spoken by very small groups. Let us consider scale.

Papua New Guinea has about 700 languages – about half the Asia-Pacific region's languages in the one country. And the differences in these languages vary from the manner of difference between German and Mandarin, to the similarity between Italian and Sicilian. Culturally, PNG is a microcosmic United Nations. Languages vary in numbers of speakers. The prize for the largest language group is claimed by the 300,000 people of the Enga province. The number of sounds used in languages varies too. The prize for the smallest number of sounds used is the language called Rotokas which is spoken by a small number of Bougainvilleans. It uses the five vowels and only six consonants.

The rich diversity of Papua New Guinea is reflected in other ways too. In the "Post-Courier" a correspondent from Port Moresby, signing himself as "A Native Son," made an eloquent reference to diversity when he sent Valentine's Day greetings to the women of Papua New Guinea"...from the ebony black of Bougainville and Mother Africa and the creamy light of Motu-Koita, Rigo, Hula circuit, Aroma and the various other parts of Papua New Guinea to all the different shades of chocolate brown all over our country and the natural blondes of Rabaul and New Ireland. God bless ... you ... and all our mothers ... on this day of love."

Papua New Guinean people typically speak three or four languages. These may include two or all three official languages plus the mother tongue, although that expression may be incorrect. Linguists talk today about the ego language, not for reasons of gender neutrality, but for reasons of its identification with the self. Tok Pisin, oblivious to the technicalities, still refers to *mama tok ples* (mother tongue)

Then if the mother and father are from different language groups, the number might be four or five. And if the maternal grandmother is from another language group, then the number might be five or six.

Developing proficiency in another language is just a part of life.

Marrying outside the language group might lead to a need

to learn the language of the in-laws. At school age a Papua New Guinean child may speak the language/s of the parents plus English at home, speak Tok Pisin in the street, and use another language with the grandparents (particularly with the grandmother), and not see this ability as anything special.

Or confusing.

***

Gabriel Babe

Gabriel Babe's name is not pronounced "babe". All consonants and vowels are pronounced in phonetic spelling. Thus Babe might be written in French as Bâbè. I deliberately make this point about French pronunciation for reasons to which I will return.

The universal adoption of phonetic spelling in Papua New Guinea means that anyone who can write and read phonetically can write and read in all languages. Understanding them is another matter.

But the adoption of the system has simplified written communication considerably.

One result is the use of an abbreviated alphabet of 22 or 23 letters. "Kw" and "eks" substitute for "q" and "x", "k" is used instead of the hard "c", and "s" replaces the soft "c". The "sh" sound is often expressed is "s", but as often as not will still appear as "sh".

"J" is often used, although is sometimes replaced with "s".

To give some examples of Australian aboriginal place names that might be written phonetically, Moonah would become Muna, Alonnah would be shortened to Alona, Woolloomooloo would shed six keystrokes to become Wulumulu, Goondiwindi would be Gundiwindi, but if the "oo" in Goondiwondi really is pronounced "u" as in cup as some Queenslanders insist, then the form Gandawindi would apply.

Ngunnawal would become Nanawol, although the purists might like to retain the "Ng" sound even though most Australians have difficulty pronouncing it.

The discussion on language would appeal to Gabriel. He speaks Nakanai, Tok Pisin, his wife's language, Mauwake (one of the Madang languages), English, and Swedish. He is now adding French to his European languages.

Gabriel is the OK Tedi Licensed Customs Agent at Tabubil. He has a Masters degree from the International Maritime College in Sweden, which he attended in 1997-98. Gabriel is from Kimbe in West New Britain, although he was born at Kavieng where his father worked at the time. It was in Sweden where Gabriel also learnt some basic French from French-speaking fellow students. He now has plans to study for his Ph D in a French-speaking country, so is studying French. But he is also thinking of Stanford as an option. No doubt some Spanish would also be useful if he were to go to California. I am sure its acquisition would not faze him at all.

Gabriel is from a family of high achievers. His father, Raki

Magao, was a Sergeant-Major in the Royal Papua New Guinea Constabulary in the 1960s. Gabriel is the third of four sons in the family. All are university graduates, of whom their father and mother are immensely proud. Gabriel talks about the considerable influence of his parents, who encouraged the behaviour and instilled the values necessary for success, and articulated their vision of a better country.

Gabriel's early education was at the Catholic Mission of the Sacred Heart at Laloka (Hoskins), followed by his high schooling at Hoskins High School. Gabriel speaks of the time he spent each day for six years walking to and from school as part of his personal investment in his education.

Gabriel's language is peppered with parables, drawing extensively and comfortably on the Catholic influence in his life, which complements his West New Britain heritage. The volume of his voice drops away theatrically as he emphasises a point.

He matriculated at the Divine Word University at Madang, where he also met his wife Elizabeth. After initially dabbling in medicine he moved into commerce, and developed his interest in transport and shipping.

The Ph D will come, but while he is sharpening up his French he is also undertaking a Bachelor of Business at the University of Southern Queensland, majoring in resource economics.

Gabriel's wide range of interests, the breadth of his education, and the strong views he has on most matters, make for challenging conversations. He is internationally travelled and well informed on issues that range across medicine, science, economics and communication. He is a Renaissance man, but locked into the perpetual rush hour of the twenty-first century.

But just as the Renaissance painters and sculptors challenged the viewer, so Gabriel challenges the listener. I do not question whether Gabriel Babe has political ambitions, but simply wonder when they might be manifested.

***

Judith Samuel

Judith Samuel's relationship with the crossword puzzle parallels that of the alcoholic with the bottle. It is tenacious. It can't be put down until it is finished, and when it is finished another is opened. I am sure if one posed the question "How many crossword puzzles a day Judith?" the answer, like the answer of the alcoholic, would be, "Do you mean how many before dinner or after?"

But in this case it is not a destructive pathology. It is Judith's way of continuing to improve her vocabulary; she describes her pursuit of words as scavenging.

To Judith, the breadth of her vocabulary is part of her stock in trade. She works with words and wears her English skills as an emblem of her profession. Since training as a secretary

Judith has worked for OTML and an international law firm in Port Moresby. She has worked within the legal and justice systems - environments that give pedantry their own special definition - so she is always a stickler for the right word and the correct process.

She tactfully corrects my Tok Pisin solecisms and pronunciation, and encourages me to do the same when she turns solecist. I can't remember it ever happening.

Judith was born on the other side of the island of New Britain from Gabriel. She is also a child of the 1960s, but her father died when she was only fourteen years old. Her mother took on the responsibility of raising the family alone and providing for their education. This is a big challenge in a country that has no formal social security system. However, the *wantok* system, and ownership of traditional land, can be described as two of the strengths of the country, ensuring a measure of equality in the distribution of resources.

Judith's mother had traditional land on Matupit. She grew traditional foods to feed the children, and grew coconuts to pay for their education. Basic needs were met. Judith's head turns away when she talks wistfully of the days when there was neither school lunch, nor money for a bus fare, and only prayers for dinner.

Through a reversal of roles, Judith is now the breadwinner. She works fulltime to provide for the needs of her mother and her children, Adele and Mary Montfort. Adele also speaks three languages, and at three Monty is already demonstrating an emerging capability in two languages.

I admire Judith's demonstration of the values and selflessness of her mother. Does a woman become her mother perhaps?

Judith Samuel's name invokes an Old Testament connection. However her values are much more New Testament – mutuality, acceptance, valuing diversity, and treating people as they would like to be treated.

***

Colin Coxswain*

Colin Coxswain has a rare facility of being able to incorporate a synonym for sexual intercourse into every phrase in every sentence. He rarely uses the word as a noun or verb, except in occasional references to management, but uses it with great dexterity in its integrated adjectival form.

The word is of uncertain origins. One theory is that the word may have its derivation in the acronym for a judicial sentence "for unlawful carnal knowledge".

Colin's ability to incorporate the integrated adjective into his language parallels that of a member of parliament deferring to "Mr Speaker" in question time. Equally his ability to revert to fluent unenhanced business English when needs be is just as impressive.

This is usually when a woman appears on the scene. This

may be as subtle as a passing whiff of perfume, but it will cause Colin to make a change of direction like the Duke of Plaza Toro going into retreat.

So great is my admiration for his ability in using the word that I can sit through meetings oblivious to the content and direction, enthralled by the diversity of meaning of this uni-bloody-versal adjective.

Its use is part of Colin's image you see. He is a blokey bloke who calls the game as he sees it, and has no difficulty in keeping in touch with his masculine side.

* His name has been changed to protect the guilty.

Wantoks and Brothers

The taxi driver in Port Moresby was from Kainantu. He is married to a woman from Wanigela on the north Papuan coast, and they have a large family, all of whom are "doing well" to use his phrase. After establishing I was from the old days and could be trusted (two unrelated considerations), he asked me about Australia, including the very direct and leading question, "Is there a *wantok* (from the English "one talk" – one language group) system in Australia".

Wantoks literally means people from the one language group. It is an extension of the notion of brother.

The *wantok* system is based on mutual obligation and support, values that have parallels in all cultures. The *wantok* system is often criticised for its very basis in the need of the community being greater than the need of the individual. However, one may wonder if this simply reflects a recognition of another reality when a comparison is made with western values.

It is also tempting to argue that the wantok system may be under long-term threat as Papua New Guinea rapidly adopts the values of the very westerners who criticise the system.

My observation is that the number of people who consider themselves *wantoks* increases with the distance from the place of birth. Thus any two people from one province who are not technically *wantoks* within the province will almost certainly consider themselves to be *wantoks* if they meet in Port Moresby. In Australia, any Papua New Guinean from any province is a wantok of any other Papua New Guinean.

One may conject as to why this is so, and ask if it dilutes the obligations and benefits that support the wantok system.

But the answer is quite simple. The need for a sense of location increases the further one is from home. The further people are from home, and the more tenuous their bonds, the greater the need to have a sense of belonging somewhere. Australians with a Papua New Guinea connection call themselves *wantoks*. Why not? It is simply using a word that describes a system of mutual understanding, support, and belonging.

Although his opening remark about the family "doing well" was in itself a statement about status and the distribution of privilege in society, I assumed that it was not a discussion about social groups that he wanted, and waited for him to lead the conversation further.

He explained that he has visited northern Australia on a couple of occasions and was surprised at the number of Papua New Guineans he saw there. "How do my *wantoks* get to live in Australia?" he went on to enquire. "Australia is an immigrant country," I offered, "Australia will take the best people from anywhere".

But as to a *wantok* system I told him that there is none in Australia. In Australia there is Alliance Française, the Celtic Club, the Returned Services Clubs, the First Fleeters, the German Harmonie Club, and the Caledonian Society. But there is no wantok system.

He seemed convinced.

***

Joel Eremugo introduces me in the Operating Excellence group as his brother. In doing so he pays me a compliment.

Joel is from Chuave in the Chimbu Province. He works for OTML as the Infrastructure Support Coordinator for Kiunga and Bige and is located at Kiunga. We were working together on a training course project relating to physical losses of copper concentrate in its handling at the Kiunga mill.

I visited Chuave on many occasions in the distant past. On the first visit in September 1963 several of us from the Port Moresby Speleological Society undertook an extensive preliminary exploration of the Kaimomo cave system. I had therefore first visited Chuave before Joel was born. Joel comments on the seniority this suggests.

In our breaks Joel talks of his occasional naughtiness as a young man, and someone "having a go" at him. Going the biff. Threatening the knuckle sandwich.

One wonders at the temerity of anyone even contemplating such an endeavour. Joel is solid. Cube shaped with the edges knocked off. Perhaps hewn from a block of highland rock - and maybe by the hand of Henry Moore. "Having a go" at Joel would seem to be a courageous endeavour.

But inside is a gentle man, whose regard for his friend is indicated by the Papua New Guinean custom of slipping his arm into mine. It is an endearing gesture not often seen in the west.

After lunch we greet each other in Kuman, although it is not Joel's language.

Greetings. Greetings, greetings. Greetings brother. Double greetings. It could be a translation from Shakespeare or Marlowe.

Joel expresses surprise that after so many years I still remember a few words of Kuman. "A few words, Joel? They are my only words".

Joel and his wife have three children. He is from a family of five, and is outnumbered by his sisters four to one; he is the boy in the middle. Do these factors contribute to his gentleness I wonder?

His father was a Lutheran pastor, who is now retired. The family lived on a mission station at Morogabi Lutheran Church on the Highlands Highway. Joel has a strong sense of connection to his birthplace.

He attended Chuave High School and went on to Lae Technical College to study fitting and machining. He was offered an apprenticeship in this field with Bougainville Copper Limited, but the Bougainville crisis began just as Joel was completing his apprenticeship.

OTML stepped in offering him a position in the milling division.

Joel displays strong leadership in his approach to dealing in abstract with the problem we are given. I admire the loyalty he demonstrates to his employer and struck by his compelling presence when reporting back to the group on our recommendations.

In calling me brother Joel is not using the word in the sense of a western family classification system. Brother in Melanesian society can have a far wider meaning. Although it generally refers to a relative of the same generation, there are occasions when there may not be a close biological connection. Little reason is seen to observe such a technicality. Indeed in the Faiwol language of Tabubil I could find no word that translates literally as sibling.

In any event, in traditional society the role of brother brings benefits and responsibilities. In some cultures an elder brother or sister may be given special privileges, but there are reciprocal obligations. A visiting elder brother or sister may be given a special room in the house, but also may be expected to provide small gifts.

Joel farewells me on the conclusion of the course with a bear hug that nearly breaks my back, and reminds me to never forget the Kuman word for brother - *angra*.

***

The *wantok* system is often criticised by westerners for its strengths of reciprocity and obligation. The nearest in the west is the network, the old school tie, and fraternity rings. And the alumni associations, professional bodies, clubs, the group with which one drinks, associating with the same consulting company, airline lounge memberships, and cultural and religious groups. But I am reliably informed these do not provide mutual support and obligation.

The driver drops me off at the Airways Hotel. He calls me wantok. I add a final few words to the answer to his question, "No, my friend, there is no *wantok* system in Australia."

Tabubil

If the heart of OTML is the mine at Mt Fubilan, and the mind is the "White House" (the colloquial name of the white painted headquarters building), then the soul has to be Tabubil. And as learned experts in earlier days were asked by enquirers, "Of what substance is the soul made?" so one may ask the same question about the soul of OTML. But unlike the learned physicians of yore who weighed bodies ante- and post-mortem to determine if the soul in fact had substance, we do not need to go to such extremes at Tabubil.

Technically Tabubil is a mine site under Papua New Guinea law, but it is the town that was built to serve the mine. It sits 600 metres above sea level on a plateau above the Ok Tedi and the Ok Menga. The site may have been part of the Hindenburg Wall a thousand ages ago, but in any event, Tabubil happily sits there between the two oks (rivers) and a very hard place.

Although there was a town plan, and there were amenity obligations to be met under the terms of the mine lease, the fact is that Tabubil was conceived not out of love, but out of necessity. The functions it had to serve were nothing more than to support the operations of the mine, to provide a dormitory for the workers, a site for the offices, a connection with the outside world, and a location for workshops and training facilities.

It was an unfortunate child, destined to wear blue singlets and elastic-sided safety boots.

How the expectation changed. Tabubil has become the biggest town in the Western Province and the location of schools and a hospital that are the envy of the rest of Papua New Guinea. At a farewell function for a senior manager at the conclusion of his contract, tears were shed in gratitude for the way in which the hospital had affected the life of this family. Nothing was said explicitly in the response to the farewell speeches, but everyone knew what was meant when the few cryptic references were made.

Tabubil - the soul of OTML - had touched these people.

It is a town of 10,000 people. It started with a camp for unaccompanied employees, and some relocatable, but otherwise permanent, accommodation for the more senior staff. Many of the houses retain their obvious origins in this architectural style of mining towns. At the centre of many homes are the steel skids on which the basic houses were bulldozed into their current position. Here they settled, were later extended, and grew comfortable in their residential plots. Gardens have been established, homes have been created, and as one family moves on and another arrives gardens are handed on to new carers, plants are bequeathed, and the rites to the betel (areca) nut harvest are proclaimed.

Occasionally the tranquility of these gardens is disturbed when the arboriophobes in Towns Administration despatch the tree fellers to remove trees that are looking slightly dangerous. Highly risk-averse is this mining business.

Tabubil is home to mine workers and mine contractors from all parts of the globe. The majority of the residents are from Papua New Guinea, but there are also people from

Australia, the Philippines, Indonesia, England, the USA, South Africa, Chile and Canada. And I have probably missed some others.

There is a commercial centre, a superstore, several specialty stores, two banks, a credit union, a Post Office, a travel agent, schools, a pharmacy, three clubs, a hotel/motel, churches, a hospital, government offices, a police station, a court, an airport, a fresh produce market, and a mess that serves 5000 meals a day. TV (all 20 channels) is received from a satellite, beamed to a ground station, and cabled into every house and all rooms in the single accommodation. It really is an immaculate reception.

Then there is the golf club. The course has "greens" of sand, and arguably is the only golf course in the world with limestone outcrops and subterranean water drains to contend with.

The Ok Tedi Mining Agreement Act also required the construction of a cinema, but the requirement flickered into obscurity with changes in entertainment technology.

Second generation Tabubil residents now work for OTML, and third generation residents attend the Tabubil schools.

A widely loved and greatly respected Australian politician was once asked "Shouldn't Canberra be more like the rest of Australia?"

"No", intoned Gough Whitlam in response, "the rest of Australia should be more like Canberra".

I cannot help thinking about Gough Whitlam every time

I make the observation that rest of Papua New Guinea should be more like Tabubil. However the reality is that although probable to imagine, it would be impossible to achieve. A nice thought though.

***

Bill Blenkhorn, Executive Manager, Logistics, systematically moves through the office, popping in to this office or that room, quickly looking at performance graphs, and addressing all of the staff by name. He asks simply, "Another perfect day in paradise?"

"Yes, Bill." has to be the response to the question. "And why", one thinks, "can't it be like this elsewhere in Papua New Guinea?"

There is an avuncular familiarity about Bill. He is the doppelganger of Jack Straw, the UK Foreign Secretary, and former Home Secretary. Like Bill Blenkhorn, Jack Straw is a strategist. Like Jack Straw, Bill Blenkorn walks a knight's move behind the boss.

Bill is one of the Canadian contingent. Originally from Nova Scotia, he plans to retire to British Columbia in the near future after thirty-five years in mining.

He has worked in copper mining in Canada, the USA, and Chile in addition to Papua New Guinea, but rarely in his two areas of technical training - surveying and geology. The wide range of sites has provided Bill with a set of reference points to compare developed and developing countries, and has lead to his view that major high profile organisations that operate in the developing world have obligations that go beyond fiduciary duty and creating shareholder value. Clearly, being profitable and successful is the first objective, as without this there can be no spin-off benefit.

There is a time in the ascent of the management tree when the need to know the right answers must give way to the need to know the right questions. I sense that Bill handled this transition well, and that it occurred relatively early in his career.

Mining is a conservative environment. OTML does such a good job of training and recruiting people to provide the right answers that it has introduced a major initiative designed to train supervisors and managers in asking the right questions.

This was a very bold move on the part of senior management.

Managers looking for change today have a variety of weapons in their arsenal. These vary from changing or redefining environments, to providing training, to tipping out the old and replacing them, to buying even higher-priced technical experts, to adopting some of the newer weapons like quality circles.

But in the environments that are inherently authoritarian and conservative, such as the military or mining, anything that smacks of the analysis of McGregor is looked upon with some suspicion. The sergeant, about to storm a hill, is unlikely to turn to the troops, produce a white board, and conduct a brainstorming session on the subject of taking hills.

The "Operating Excellence" initiative was brilliant in its concept. It was about technical experts, initially employed to know the answers, learning how to ask questions. It was about turning problems over and looking at them from the other side. It was about adopting new ways of thinking. But first the people had to learn how to change the way they think.

The intention was that this program would provide a kick-start for a "future state" organisation. Old business models tend to leave many people in the organisation under-utilised, not in terms of knowing the standard answers but in knowing the questions that will trigger the new ideas.

Bill always knew the right questions.

***

Mining is a conservative industry. It is simply about moving earth, removing minerals, and moving the earth back again. And the earth moves for many people on Saturday night in Tabubil when visitors to the men's and women's single quarters do not have the distraction of the usual 10 pm curfew.

But the OTML phenomenon is more than a mine. It is not just about changing the shape of a mountain and the extraction of minerals.

It is about a company that has made mistakes, but has learnt from them. It has made a lot of money, but has contributed substantially to the local and broader Papua New Guinea economies. Dr Roger Higgins on the eve of his departure emphasised that 93% of the wealth created by

OTML remains in Papua New Guinea, and that 82% equity remains in the country.

With mine closure only a few years away, the company has put in place a strategy that will ensure a level of funding for the ongoing development of infrastructure in Western Province for forty years on. Tabubil will be the centre for this development. Bill Blenkhorn's vision of orderliness in the phasing out of the old and the phasing in of the new will be realised.

Tabubil's role will broaden from providing support for mining operations. It is a role that is still being discussed. Maybe it could become a university town. All major universities in Australia now have campuses in the Asia Pacific Region. Why not Tabubil as a centre of excellence in adventure tourism, eco-tourism and multi-cultural studies?

The OTML story is about improvements in the lifestyle of the local people, reduction in the incidence of debilitating illness, extending life expectancy, undertaking research into improving food crops, and reducing infant mortality. It is about remediating an environmental mistake. It is about a social conscience, a generous employee-housing scheme, building a local supplier capability, educating a workforce, and contributing extensively to the Western Province infrastructure through the construction of roads, airports, hospitals, schools and police stations through the Papua New Guinea government's Tax Credits Scheme. And more than a handful of former OTML employees have become members of the Papua New Guinea parliament.

These are products of the soul of OTML as much as the heart; products of the people who live in Tabubil.

OTML could be the corporate model the government of a developing country might endorse - building the skills base needed to capitalise on a resource, seeking ways to equitably distribute wealth for the common good, and recruiting the best staff from around the world.

***

Areas of commercial activity that affect most of the town residents include the banks, the retail stores, and the Post Office.

Retail banking in Papua New Guinea has a set of rules that bewilder, but seem to work.

Although rapidly being e-enabled, Papua New Guinea banking at retail level is still face-to-face, thus allowing the bank to have meaningful dialogue with the customers who are now largely ignored in other countries.

A weeklong communications blackout at Tabubil illustrated just how dependent the system is on its electronic communications, notwithstanding the apparent paper war.

Queuing is necessary to manage the numbers, paralleling in a sense being "on hold" for telephone banking in other countries.

But the queues are not as organised, nor the people as compliant, as would be found in the UK or even Australia. In the UK queuing has a set of rules that would confuse a crowd of sociologists. However, in Tabubil, queues are no more than a loose grouping of customers, hangers-on and sightseers.

Tellers attend to multiple customers at once. I wonder how they get a balance at the end of the day as they simultaneously count the cash of a large business deposit, process a smart card withdrawal between counting the 50s and the 20s, sell a draft between counting the 20s and the tens, and then tend to a queue jumper who seeks change for the telephone, before returning to the business deposit.

I'm confused; how is the teller coping?

Documents are completed with more flourishes than an illuminated manuscript, and fingers pound out a paradiddle on the counter to punctuate the departure of each customer and the arrival of the next.

Banking is undertaken far too impersonally in other countries today.

Queuing in supermarkets has a set of associated inevitabilities that are common the world over. So there is a sense of Safeway at the Tabubil Superstore where there are queues for the dozen checkouts. The universal truths? Simply that the queue that appears to be the shortest isn't, that "express lane" is an oxymoron, and that the change will run out the moment my purchases are scanned and I tender my kina.

The range of 7000 lines carried compares favourably

with supermarkets anywhere around the world. One obvious difference however is in the small packages, bottles and sachets of products that are provided to meet the need of people who may have to walk some kilometres home, and the limited storage facilities for perishables once they get there. They also reflect the high level of ticket resistance that is now common in retail in PNG, where a weak currency and long supply lines have put even the most essential of imports beyond the reach of many.

***

Tracey Kiliwo

The sign in the MAF terminal at Tabubil advises passengers in a mixture of Tok Pisin and English of a "*bikpela tambu tru long karim extra cargo olsem kakaruk, plastic, bag, bilum na ol kain samting olsem ikam tru long loading gate or security gate*" (Carrying extra hand cargo such as chickens, plastic shopping bags, bags and handbags through the loading gate or security gate is prohibited).

I am at the MAF terminal at Tabubil enquiring about a flight to Telefomin at the weekend. Tracey Kiliwo, a Telefol, is particularly helpful. Telefomin does not have a phone service, so she uses the radio to enquire of her counterpart at the Telefomin airport as to the availability of a room at one of the local guesthouses. The Baptist Mission guesthouse is already booked out, but she is able to find me an alternative for K60 a night - no breakfast

As to the times of flights, Tracey is similarly helpful. She books me on the last flight out of Tabubil to Telefomin on the Friday, and the first flight out of Telefomin to Eliptamin and Tabubil on the Monday.

I enquire about flight times. "There are no scheduled times," Tracey informs me. "The last flight out will leave when all the other runs are complete. The first flight out on Monday morning will be at first light."

How wonderfully anarchic it is. How heart-warming that MAF is able to eschew the adoption of computerised schedules and ticketing systems and that there is a situation with which the booking systems used by the big airlines could not cope.

Tracey's assistance is exemplary too. Imagine the hope-renewing experience of a real person serving a customer without the anonymity of a 1300 phone number, and Tracey going out of her way to find me accommodation. It is an experience of true Papua New Guinea hospitality.

Evelyn Mongse

Eva works for Tabubil-based Camp Administration Ltd in a customer service role. I call her the Director of First Impressions. Camp Administration Ltd is a locally-owned emporium – Tabubil's Bunnings. Eva works on the front desk, plays tunes on the computer, takes money, remembers names, and balances cash.

The diminutive, ever smiling, Eva is Oksapmin-born. She was educated at the Telefomin High School, and English was the language of her education. Oksapmin is her traditional language, and she also speaks Tok Pisin.

It is Eva's first year at work, and she has taken on the huge responsibility of paying for the education of her brother Dekit.

Eva accepts without question the role of family bread-winner, but it is a daunting responsibility for someone so young. Eva has high aspirations in life, but for the moment is happy to consolidate where she is, and see Dekit through his third year of Mechanical Engineering at Unitech Lae.

Like so many people in Papua New Guinea, Eva has experienced the tough side of life. The experience is often called "character-building", but there is a tug at the heartstrings when Eva tells me that her mother died when she was very young, and as hard as she tries, she "can't remember her face".

***

Christine Mangen

Tina works for Starwest Constructions Limited in Tabubil and has what many at Starwest will consider being the most important job – she is the senior payroll clerk.

The daughter of Sergeant Mangen Numboin of Niagara village on the Sepik River, Christine saw a lot of Papua New Guinea as a child when her father was on postings to Hengenofi, Kainantu, Madang, Ambunti, and Aitape.

Christine recalls few details of those days, except her father's good relationship with the *kiaps* (the patrol officers). It is now twenty years since Mangen Numboin died, but he lives on in the values Christine and her two brothers and two sisters demonstrate.

Their mother, Mu, was from Sinasina in the Chimbu Province, so two Papua New Guinea languages were spoken at home, plus English. Mangen Numboin did not live to experience all the achievements of his children, but Mu survived him by sixteen years, seeing the successes that Mangen missed.

Christine Mangen attended Business College, but an emerging awareness that she had a creative side, together with the independence her father had taught her, drew her to Arts College. (Is it common to all cultures that creative arts are not taken seriously, and that one needs something "to fall back on"?)

After studying acting and traditional and modern dance for two years, Christine taught drama and movement for another year. She was a member of the Wewak Raun Isi Art Theatre that successfully brought the traditional Trobriand Island story "Sail of the Midnight Sun" to audiences around Papua New Guinea.

Now the mother of a son who is looking to his own career, Christine Mangen expresses all the concerns of today's parent. The protectiveness she learnt from her father has to be balanced with the need to let go, and her son, Michael, is now attending the College of Development Studies in Wewak, majoring in computing studies. She visits him regularly.

Starwest Constructions Limited works very closely with Ok Tedi Mining Limited. In the argot of modern management, they work in partnership, each needing the other in a symbiotic way.

Major corporate organisations today operating in a global environment look outwardly and internationally to learn. Tina, still relatively new to Starwest, has adopted this value of today's transnational, and regularly visits Australia where she travels extensively.

***

Jenny Kamai

Back in 1949 when Oscar Hammerstein II wrote the words for the song Honey Bun in the musical South Pacific, he described her as "she's just sixty inches high" (152 centimetres in today's measures, but I don't know that the song has been updated).

On the many occasions when I run into Jenny I am immediately reminded of Hammerstein's lyrics; I can't help it. Although Jenny is probably less than "sixty inches" high, she is all heart, like Honey Bun herself.

Jenny is Awin from Tmolenai village, not far from the international border. Her first language is Awin, but like most of the Awin speakers she also speaks Tok Pisin and reasonable Hiri Motu and "Malay" (Indonesia Bahasa). She also speaks English of course, the language of her education, and the language of formal business.

After attending Kiunga High School, and later the Kiunga Vocational Centre, Jenny moved to Tabubil. This was a logical and predictable move given her retail and hospitality studies at the Vocational Centre, and Tabubil being an eminently livable town and the economic centre of the Province.

Since then she has worked it "hungry" as they say in taxi parlance – fitting in as many jobs as she can in one day, seeking that main chance. She has worked at the Superstore on check-outs and the Kai Bar, and has also worked as a table waiter at the Golf Club. She also fits in some childcare for relatives just down the road from my house, so running into her as she darts from one job to another is inevitable.

We have occasional, but fleeting, conversations on the corner opposite the single women's dongas about "ships and shoes and sealing wax". Then the conversation tends to drift to how she is going (life's a battle), the dance on Saturday night (it was at the Hash last week), and how things are at home (tough).

Jenny is just 23, but already she carries the equivalent of a lifetime's experience. She has particular family obligations to meet as she is in that privileged position in Papua New Guinea – she is in formal employment.

In Australia we would describe Jenny as a battler out of respect for the way in which she rises to her challenges. If her endeavours are generally reflective of the collective capability and energy of young people in Papua New Guinea working within a political leadership vacuum, one can only wonder at how quickly and how far Papua New Guinea would leap ahead with vision and a sense of collective leadership.

At the moment I sense that many young people like Jenny – the ordinary people of Papua New Guinea – feel not just let down, but abandoned.

***

Monica Rau

"I want you to close your eyes and imagine you are a village woman in the middle of the jungle in Papua New Guinea".

"Imagine you have two young children".

Dr Monica Rau, a senior scientist with OTML was addressing a public forum in San Francisco. She was accompanied by Dr Ross Smith, then the Environment Department Chief Scientist.

"Imagine one of your children taking ill. The nearest aid post is two days walk away. But there is an alternative. If you can get a message through to OTML and they can despatch a helicopter you can cover the same ground in an hour."

Dr Rau went on to explain that OTML provided a helicopter to the village woman, and a child's life was saved. It provided a helicopter as a service to a fellow traveller on the planet. There was no question of charging.

Monica Rau uses the story to help explain that the issues around mining in a developing country are complex. Rarely is there ever an "either/or". Without OTML there would have been no helicopter and the child's life would have been lost. In some remote areas of the Star Mountains, tradition was that a child was not named until it was aged two - prior to OTML commencing mining operations it had only a limited chance of surviving that long.

Monica relates to the story at a personal level. She grew up in a village and has a family of her own – her husband Charles Tenakanai, and their two boys, Robert aged 11, and Charles aged 9. She was educated by French nuns on Yule Island in Papua. Here the French influence is strong and names like Monique are common baptismal names. Monique became Monica, partly reflecting the PNG phonetic spelling.

After taking an honours degree in science at the University of Papua New Guinea, Monica went to Oxford, completing first a Masters degree and then a Ph D. She is one of Papua New Guinea's most highly credentialled and respected scientists.

Monica is not an apologist for OTML, and indeed she will criticise where and when it is appropriate. But it is the criticism of the objective scientist, and she uses facts to support her position. She has little time for political correctness, especially if it supported by nothing weightier than urban mythology, or highly charged with righteous indignation.

Monica is the Senior Scientist, Terrestrial Programs, with responsibility for all the vegetation impacts along the river – food, trees, vegetation types, and dieback. Much of her work is involved with reforestation. Like many she will talk of the

Tedi as a habitat, a system, or a source of energy. She will talk of the pollution that is being remediated, and she will talk of the Tedi's role as a tributary of the great Fly River.

But her passion becomes most compelling when she lifts the discussion to the metaphysical, and endows the river with a life, a soul, feelings and emotions. She talks about it as an organic being rather than simply a source of energy, or water, or a habitat.

Monica is deeply religious, but not just because of her childhood on Yule Island. Like many scientists who have grappled with the great questions that can never be answered she believes totally in some greater force than we know; something we cannot understand. Monica has a strong belief that in life, physical, spiritual, and mental dimensions need to be in balance. Like all three legged stools, hers also will topple if one of the legs is not there.

She talks of the need for balance in the attitude that is demonstrated towards the Tedi. She talks of the "core of truth in all the functions it performs", but demonstrates a profound sadness that everyone, including governments and lawyers, wants to pursue river-related issues in their terms. She is saddened that no one sees the river as having a life, feelings, or a character of its own. "It cannot speak; it cannot pursue its own interests; it is the loser. People can speak and get compensation. Governments and shareholders can speak and count the economic returns. The river cannot speak". Monica senses that it is suffering a terrible sadness.

***

Bob and Susan Boerma

Bob and Susan Boerma are rarities in Tabubil. Residents for sixteen years and ten years respectively, they are the only foreigners I know who consider Tabubil to be home. Indeed, Tabubil is their only home. They love Papua New Guinea's most livable town.

Arriving in January 1987, Bob quickly settled into both the mining environment and the Lions Club of Tabubil, where he held most offices over the following years. He also spent two years as Chairman of the Boy Scouts Fund Committee, drawing on his earlier experience in Canada where he worked with the Boy Scouts for many years.

Having several trades, and with a background in construction and manufacturing in Canada, Bob fitted in well to his role at OTML in community development. Such is the high esteem in which the local people regard Bob that village leaders in the region lobbied for him to continue now that news of his retirement has been announced. It will be a reluctant retirement.

Bob and Susan married in 1993. Susan complements Bob in many ways. A commerce graduate, and a former corporate executive with Bacnotan Cement Consolidated Industries in the Philippines, Susan needed an outlet in Tabubil so she created a magnificent garden – arguably the best in town. She also learnt to cook, and has developed a fine set of skills that many of the people of Tabubil have come to appreciate, and always look forward to experiencing again. I certainly did.

The social highlight of Tabubil is Bob and Susan's Saturday night dinners. These provide a canvas for their rich combination of creative and aesthetic skills – Susan's in the kitchen, and Bob's as a furniture craftsman in the wide range of beautiful timbers of the Western Province. Bob is vocal in his concern at the export of these timbers with no value-added activity conducted locally and no benefit accruing to the people of the Western Province, particularly the people of the Wawoi River area. Against the back drop of the garden, the picture comes together, and one appreciates why the Boermas share a passion for their adopted home.

Great effort is invested in pursuing the right combination of guests, and seating arrangements. I do believe that the Boerma household is one of very few in Tabubil where foreign residents have a meaningful opportunity for a social get together with Papua New Guineans.

Bob's retirement is imminent. Bob and Susan will be missed, as they will also miss Tabubil.

***

Nina

Nina was born in Bolobip. Her language is Faiwol, one of the several languages of the Min area of Papua New Guinea.

She has a simple discrete tattoo on her left cheek bone (rendered on the bank of a river, using lampblack and sap from flowers). It has no specific meaning, but it subtly complements the fair complexion she shares with many of the Min people. Nina is very matter of fact in the way she describes her village, the gardens, the food, the mountains, and the rest houses on the two-day walk home.

But today it's a global village, and there are tensions and contradictions to confuse her. Nina attended High School as a boarder for four years, and has completed year 10. She is eighteen, and has spent almost a quarter of her life away from the daily influence of home.

And like eighteen-year-old girls the world over, she knows what is happening on the pop scene in America, follows what is universally trendy among teenagers, is an avid television viewer, and can express the same challenging attitude through the way the baseball cap or the hipster jeans are worn.

Nina is smart and knowledgeable in a way that indicates a broader learning experience than just formal schooling. She is very animated, strongly independent, and speaks idiomatic English with the same fluency and accent as everyone who has grown up in a multi-cultural environment where American television is the major window into the other world.

She describes my house as "very cool". Provocatively, I ask if she would like me to turn the air-conditioning down.

Nina is at a cross roads, and I am helping her write a resume in case the turn she takes is into the workplace rather than back to school to complete years 11 and 12. Nina is bright, and recognises that Papua New Guinea is very unforgiving to the under-educated. My counsel is to go back to school and use her obvious talents; year 12 is necessary for higher education.

On top of that the additional couple of years would give her more exposure to the technology of the workplace today. Not that Nina will have any trouble with the technology. Generation Y and with the techno-savvy associated with it, Nina picks up the remote control of my television, tells me the time, sets the alarm (what time do you like to wake up in the morning?) and plays some games, in between flicking through the movie channels, giving me the details the resume requires, and supping on a beer with ice.

Over that is the incessant chatter. Her interests are as eclectic as those of any teenager already an adult but not yet having the responsibilities that go with it: boys, makeup, hanging out, cool, and expressing an opinion on most matters. Like all interactions one has with people of this age group, it is an experience that is energising one moment, enervating the next, and ultimately exhausting.

Nina is staying with her mother tonight. She leaves to walk home. Her bilum (a traditional string bag for food) is slung over the baseball cap in cultural counterpoint. The young body is a lot tauter than that of an eighteen-year-old from the outside cultures that have a major influence on her. She leans into the bilum; her abs assume the definition of an athlete's. She opens her umbrella and walks into the darkness of the wet night with an elegant and confident glide, unafraid.

Nina is eighteen; she has no fear.

Tabubil Street Names

The names of many of the Tabubil streets are Faiwol or Wopkai words (two of the Min languages). As in Mount Hagen, the street names have become a major connection with the local languages.

There is some confusion where similar words in the two languages have different meanings. However the following translations are provided for any residents of Tabubil who may not have had the opportunity to explore the meanings of the street names. The translations provided have been checked and rechecked, but I am not totally confident about their accuracy.

I sense that initially some of the names may have been suggested as a joke, which certainly was the impression that came through in trying to have them translated. I also found that some of the street names (which I have left out) apparently translate into words usually described in dictionaries as ***vulg***. As tempting as it is to liberate such words from the gulags whence they are usually consigned, I have decided to err on the side of family values and the language of polite company.

It is also possible my translators were "just having a lend of me".

Aket	heart
Atam	lizard
Atan	sun
Awon	bird
Bakan	ground or earth
Betin	waterfall
Bitimil	lake
Dai	die
Dakon	an edible leaf
Dukum	big
Imal	limestone cave
Kam	blood
Karal	wife
Kabil	trap
Kayop	moon
Kinum	man
Kumsip	cassowary
Lokoloko	up the mountain
Mamus	leader or chief
Menga	a place name
Min	son, or people
Namal	white
Nogum	wantok
Nuk	cuscus
Tanabal	orphan in one language; good in the other
Takam	a fish
Tapa	tapa cloth
Tum	stone

Shin	sin
Wakaum	a bird of paradise
Wangum	sap of the kaukau
Wok	water
Wopkai	a clan name
Wom	sago
Yaman	taro
Yereng	spear

*****

Mine Closure

Mine closure may be only a few years away, and OTML has done the unusual in mining. The copper and gold will run out in a few years (the number of years varies as data are developed), and OTML has put in place a number of a strategies that will ensure that it leaves behind more than a vacuum.

The boldest of these strategies is the incorporation of a company that will continue to support the development of infrastructure in the Western Province for forty years after closure. The PNG Sustainable Development Program Limited (PNGSDPL) will manage a fund that has been accumulated from recurrent profits. The PNGSDPL, whose board has a broad range of management and development skills, will allocate funds to specific projects, ensuring that the developmental momentum initiated by OTML in the Province is not lost.

The PNGSDPL has been incorporated in Singapore for two reasons. The first is that Singapore has a more investment-friendly environment than Papua New Guinea. The second is the view that a substantial geographical distance between the Papua New Guinea government and the funds will mitigate the risk of a future government taking control and transferring funds to consolidated revenue.

There is a view that some governments in Papua New Guinea's history have demonstrated a lack of capability to manage finances in the long-term, and that various sources, such as the National Provident Fund, have been looted to meet a budget deficit or to finance sectional interests. Whilst these actions may have been the actions of the desperate, and possibly were well intentioned, the result is regarded as having been at the cost to the little person, and to the benefit of the leaders.

There will also be a need to kick start subsistence agriculture, warnings about which were given in the past. Beefing up OTML's research into food crops will be part of this.

In April 1979 the Papua New Guinea government's Ok Tedi Coordinator visited Kieta, Arawa, and Panguna, with a view to observing changes that had occurred with the development of copper mining on Bougainville, and ask what one could learn from the Bougainville experience that might apply to Ok Tedi.

There was a concern that Ok Tedi might be the echo chamber of Bougainville Copper Limited.

With this in mind, Chris Warrillow, an experienced former field officer in the Australian administration of PNG and by now an adviser to the Papua New Guinea government, took a clinical look at what was occurring in Bougainville, recorded his observations, and drew his conclusions.

Many of Warrillow's observations were about the long term effect on traditional life. Clearly, development in an environment characterised by a huge inflow of cash would be to the detriment of subsistence agriculture.

The need to return to local agriculture after mine closure, will also require early planning. The experience in Bougainville tells us that the lead time can be measured in years.

Tabubil will be the centre for this management of the

development of the Western Province.

***

Another strategy is the Shares in Success Scheme

It was a 19th century Neapolitan by the name of Tonti who is regarded as the first person to propose a financial scheme by which benefits accrue to those who hang on longest. He gave his name to what became known as a tontine.

A tontine, conceived by OTML in the hope that money alone would stem the hemorrhage of key personnel, may have been the wrong answer to a sensible question; a question asked with the best of intent, "How do we arrest the exodus of key foreign staff, and retain them until mine closure?"

Part of the response to the question was a scheme – Shares in Success – that would be paid as an additional benefit to those who stayed on until mine closure. It resulted immediately in a degree of cynicism among employees. Funded by a percentage allocation of annual nett profits, the SISS idea overlooked two important realities, firstly that Papua New Guinea has a largely negative expatriate employment image – high tax, frontier image and a reputation for lawlessness – and does not provide a supportive foreign employment climate, and secondly the principle that the more talented, and therefore the most mobile, staff are usually the first to leave.

I am not suggesting longer-term employees lack the capability to find alternative jobs. Indeed I would propose that the core of these people – foreigners and Papua New Guineans alike – are highly regarded internationally, and are some of the best, and most dedicated, people with whom I have ever worked.

There might have been other issues too. One I sensed was that to some senior foreigners the context of their work was mining – it was purely incidental that the mine was in PNG. The consequence is a cultural dissociation.

There is little sense of engagement by the foreigners with the people of Papua New Guinea. Building communications, learning a new language, and understanding culture are rarely pursued, and generous off-site field breaks emphasise the negative side of working in Papua New Guinea.

Taking field breaks at Papua New Guinea destinations would help build the sense of context, and those co-workers I encouraged to take local leave marvelled at the experience, whether walking the Kokoda Track, visiting Milne Bay or visiting a resort on New Ireland.

The continuing healthy growth of the Australian economy and the consequential shortage of skills in Australia cannot be ignored. This is so significant today that Australian companies have to actively recruit staff from overseas to feed the demand, and industry associations are looking at ways of encouraging the return of the one million or so Australian expatriates working outside the country.

With a formal workforce of only 6% of the Papua New Guinea population, the tax burden falls on only 300,000 people, including the 1800 well-paid employees of OTML. It is tempting for the government to increase personal taxation levels, but with rumours that the top marginal tax rate was to increase from 50% to 60%, with 75% being mooted for the longer term, it was no surprise that foreign staff were leaving at a rate greater than the capacity to replace them.

Another issue, that work permits for Papua New Guinea are issued by grace and favour of the government, does not make for long-term employment stability. Upsetting someone in power – perhaps a politician – may just result in a word in the right ear in Port Moresby, and the withdrawal of a work permit.

But OTML is in a position of power too. With less than 1% of Papua New Guinea's formal workforce, it produces 10% of the Papua New Guinea GDP. OTML's copper concentrate export is so significant to the Papua New Guinea economy that the value of the kina appears to moves synchronously with the depth of the Fly River. In the dry season when the product cannot be exported the value of the kina falls as a result.

SISS will be a huge windfall to those who choose to stay on. Demand for copper will explode with the burgeoning markets in China and India and prices and profits will skyrocket. Those who stay on to take advantage of SISS will share in a handsome windfall.

The employees who have an eye on mine closure are not standing still either. Many are preparing for life after the mine with business pursuits of their own. The business rigour they have learnt at OTML will give them a head start as they move into agricultural pursuits, trading ventures, and in two examples at least, what appear to be possible bed and breakfast ventures that can be kicked into gear as soon as Papua New Guinea's reputation of being an unsafe destination for tourists is turned around, and Papua New Guinea takes its rightful place as a major tourist destination in the region.

Agriculture has a special significance in these plans, with the concentration being on cocoa, oil palm and vanilla for export, but some are pursuing betel nut (for domestic consumption).

Like so much tropical agriculture, there is little opportunity for post-harvest value adding. The principal differentiators in the market are quality, price and proximity to markets (with related price implications). Coffee, cocoa and tea have been grown since the 50s and 60s, and the introduction of palm oil in the 60s gave a fillip to national agricultural income figures.

Palm oil has a bright future with the huge demand of the Chinese market. Ironically it was UK interests drove the development of the palm oil industry in Papua New Guinea. Trials with vanilla commenced in the 50s and 60s, and a generation later it is being assiduously pursued as a high unit value crop, of high quality, and with a healthy demand. International demand for cocoa is strong, and the Papua New Guinea product is regarded as being of a high quality.

A focus on the resources sector took the spotlight away from agriculture for some years and even today annual agricultural export figures continue to show a downward trend.

With the confidence that comes from looking longer term, three families with whom I worked very closely have taken seriously their preparations for mine closure.

Allan and Cathy Bird are both second-generation OTML employees, and their three children were born at Tabubil. Despite the strong locational bonds that this suggests, they were one of the first families to make an early departure for their vanilla farm in the Sepik.

Malakai and Colleen Dam and their three children Elian, Lydia, and Mark are all from the East Sepik Province. Their plans are relatively longer term than the Birds', and they have no plans to depart early.

Colleen was brought up in West New Britain, so it was no surprise that they chose to acquire an oil palm block in West New Britain.

They talk of the flow-on benefits to the local economy that have followed the extensive plantings in West New Britain. These are in harvesting (largely a manual activity) and transporting product.

Roland Huambukie and his wife Cathline, also from the Sepik, are in their seventh year with OTML. They have six children, Joppa, Edna, Haggain, Gestina, Leah and Miseline. They are growing vanilla, and Roland is pursuing end-user markets rather than intermediary markets.

Like the Dams, the Huambukies have no plans to depart early. They speak supportively of the calibre of the OTML management team and the leadership being demonstrated.

However, the time will come, and as with other employees making their plans for trade stores, public transport pursuits, tourist accommodation, and plantations of betel nut, coconuts and cocoa, they are demonstrating uncharacteristic long term planning. They deserve to do well.

The Young Professionals

OTML invests heavily in the training and nurturing of people to support organisational needs, spending over K7 million ($AU3 million) a year on the development of its human capital. There are many measures of its commitment, such as the vigorous apprenticeship scheme in which a large number of women participate, and OTML-sponsored higher education opportunities.

Papua New Guinean people make up 95% of the workforce. There is an obligation under the OTML legislation to give employment preference to local area people, who now make up 40% of the workforce at OTML.

Positions at the highest level are held by Papua New Guineans, and all positions held by foreigners are subject to a localisation program that sets specific targets. Much of the training and development of Papua New Guinea people is specifically directed towards this objective.

Women are well represented in the workforce, accounting for around 25% of the total. Whether the glass ceiling has been broached or not remains a moot point even though an increasing level of balance in the sexes may have been achieved. There are several factors at play here - environmental, cultural, and the "catch up" factor, which is the simple reality with which all cultures have to deal.

The environmental issue is that mining is a "blokey" industry. It's about "boys and their toys". Despite the relatively high numbers of women, senior decision-makers largely are men. Whether there is a cause and effect, women tend to not be selected for higher-level development opportunities. An example was in the Operating Excellence training workshops conducted in my first few weeks on site. In the nominations for the first workshop there were twenty men and no women. Participants commented on this imbalance, so two women were nominated for the second workshop. A significant step for womankind.

Despite the huge investment in training and development, there is as yet no senior women's network group sponsored by OTML. Sponsors of government programs in Australia like Senior Women in Management (SWIM) have demonstrated a considerable return on investment from this form of personal development. However in a conservative environment where the focus of "training" tends to be on classroom activity rather than on the most appropriate learning process that will deliver the desired outcome, the benefits of OTML-sponsored networking are yet to be appreciated and achieved. However the sponsoring of a secretaries' group, and positively promoting the involvement of secretaries in the national Secretary of the Year event is a significant and useful start.

There is a sensitive cultural issue in the advancement of women in the company. Women speak of the effect on family dynamics if a woman is promoted above the level of the husband. Indeed some women attribute pressure on their marriages, and marital breakdown, to this very point. They also suggest that in a subliminal reaction to this possibility, senior managers at OTML may tend to favour promoting a man over a woman.

There may be no evidence to support the proposition, but in the event that it may occur occasionally, my sympathy is with the decision-maker who is probably trying to play the impossible game, balancing a handful of competing pressures, and turning infinite shades of grey into black and white.

The inherent conservativeness of the mining industry is also reflected in the absence of gender-neutral language. As an issue this is passé in Australia, and I daresay it only grates on those who have seen the changes in other environments. There is also an apparent tension with first-point-of-contact roles. A senior woman will generally be nominated to "fill in" on the reception counter ahead of a junior man.

In a conservative industry in a culturally-conservative country it is women's work.

The final issue, which is catch up, is a simple reality that has to be acknowledged. Papua New Guinea is a young country that has come a long way in a short time. Traditional values give strength and stability, so by necessity change will be slow. This has also been a reality in western countries over many generations as tradition has been challenged, and society has stirred and shed some of the past. This is neither good nor bad; it is just a reality.

But the positive side is that the cadre of what I call the young professionals is as talented and enthusiastic as one will find anywhere. These people have a huge responsibility in the development of their country.

***

Bill Wangi

Bill is Mr Helpful. Nothing's a problem, and he gave me enormous assistance on my arrival, cobbling together a computer for me. Originally pedal-powered I suspect, but possibly steam-driven, and the only known example of a Windows '81 operating system left in captivity, it provided Bill with some challenges. But he used his talents to craft a hard drive, and to "arrange" an uninterruptible power supply so we would not have to put the machine to a potentially fatal power supply test.

Bill spent time in the Papua New Guinea Navy as an electronics technician, gaining his electronics certificate in the two years he spent in the late 1980s on secondment to the Australian Navy. So he was a dab hand when it came to the technical challenges like de-fragmenting the hard drive, jury-rigged though it was.

Bill's naval background had some unusual consequences. He stood rather than sat at a dinner party for the single staff (it was all that time on the bridge he claimed).

He also has the most abstemious habits, and the most admirable self-discipline - for a sailor.

Now the Regional Logistics Coordinator at Kiunga, and able to bring his family to site, Bill and his wife Theresia (who comes from Manjin Kwarui village, in the Wosera Area of the East Sepik Province) will soon have their family with them. With ages ranging from fifteen down to the two-year old twins, there are Gideon, Violet Kramrik, Hembenngua, Siborah, Emma, Sengiwai, Javiwai, Sengisause, and Twinava and Twineri.

***

Edward Houwo

There is a libel in the riddle -

Q What is the difference between an accountant and a com puter?
A. The computer is the one with the personality.

It is libelous, because all the accountants I know, particularly those who are close friends, are larger-than-life characters with all of the personality needed to be the centre of the party.

Edward Houwo is in this group.

Edward trained as an accountant and is a graduate of the Divine Word University in Madang. He is from Asaro in the Eastern Highlands Province, or as Eddie says, "Mudman Country".

He is big in style and personality, and has all the accoutrements of the accountant - the symbols of office. The laptop on which he can rustle up a spreadsheet in an instant; the first in the group to have an e-mail address at home; the Walkman; the sunnies pushed onto the top of his head.

Edward initially worked as a contracts administrator, responsible for the suite of Transport contracts - ship, helicopter and aircraft chartering, stevedoring services, and motor vehicle maintenance. It was a considerable suite of work that required that Edward develop literacy in law, engineering, transport and other professional and technical fields.

After a 12-month sabbatical back in Mudman Country Edward returned to Ok Tedi as Contracts Officer for the wide range of Provincial infrastructure contacts undertaken by OTML under the Papua New Guinea government's Tax Credit Scheme.

His wife Theresa, also from Asaro, is another young professional. Theresa was educated at the Onamuga Health Training Centre in Kainantu, in The Eastern Highlands Province. Today she is a nurse who works at the Goroka hospital as a Community Health Worker and works in the Antenatal Clinic on matters such as family planning, welfare of families, and healthy living in the community. As Edward says, "Similar to Pat's work in Mount Hagen in the early days".

They have three sons, Joshua (5), Caleb (3) and Gershom who is one year old. Edward and Theresa take their parenting responsibilities seriously, building the foundations for the future.

***

Caroline Kereku

Caroll Kereku personifies the management maxim that you should always give an urgent job to a busy person.

Caroll joined the company in 1994 as a graduate recruit fresh from the University of Papua New Guinea, and was widely seen to be a rising star. She was the human resources coordinator for the Logistics Division when I arrived, and following a major restructure she was co-opted to one of the transition teams.

She is tall, with an imposing presence. At the risk of making a generalisation about the Tolai people, the contribution they have made to the development of Papua New Guinea must be admired. Caroll sits well in the company of the Tolai leaders that include Prime Ministers, politicians, knights of the realm, doctors, teachers, and the successful business people who have made their mark on Papua New Guinea.

Caroll suffers no fools. In a meeting the glasses slide slowly down the nose until she peers over them. She stares down at the opposition like a schoolteacher. But when the point is made, the glasses are pushed back to the bridge of her nose, and her face creases with a smile that is sure to win over any opponent.

Caroll is also Secretary of the Golf Club, and the mother of a young daughter. Each could be a full time job on its own. The Golf Club is a central social feature in Tabubil, and membership exceeds 100. One can imagine Caroll in a committee meeting, glasses sliding further down the nose, until she wins the game.

Everyone's friend and mentor, Caroll stops to talk in the office, at the superstore, or at the golf club, whether it is a social greeting, a report on a development in her project, or dispensing advice. She has a generous Melanesian heart, and has happily taken on the responsibility of a six-week old baby who has been left in her care; it was literally a foundling left on her front door step. Into a little life the light of love had shone.

Caroll is the daughter of Damien Kereku, a well-known East New Britain political figure. I expect one day Damien will be known as Caroll's father.

Post script. The light went out on a Sunday night in Tabubil when Caroll met her appointment in Samarra. It was a single car crash. It was a wet night and there no suspicious circumstances; it may have been the camber of the road, or a rush to get to her next meeting. It was devastating news the next morning, particularly to those who had been with her the previous evening.

The town-wide question was "How could it be? How could this happen to someone of such obvious goodness?"

With no obvious answers, there was conjecture about bad spirits taking away the friend to all.

Damien spoke at his daughter's funeral and his tears were shared. The town formally mourned Caroll's death for two weeks.

***

Michael Guba

A senior manager in a major transnational company in Australia taught me a lot about recruitment and the need to consider people's competencies, attitude, and their indefinable "interestingness", rather than just technical knowledge and skills.

I could never talk to Michael without acknowledging that he qualifies on the dimensions of "interestingness". Michael also took on the personal challenge of helping me re-learn Hiri Motu, which I took on with greater alacrity than skill.

Michael Guba trained in horticultural science; he is an agricultural extension officer. He works as a senior cataloguer in procurement now, but it is not surprising that he gravitated to cataloguing as a lot of horticulture is about the same science of systematic order; of taxonomy. He maintains a particular interest in horticulture. He is the resident expert in such matters and can identify a fruiting betel nut palm at 200 paces.

"That flower is a relative of ginger," he offers. His diagnosis of the knobs on a lime is "probably a virus". (In Australia, I usually have to produce my Medicare card to get that advice.) "Look at this flower", he says when we run into each other at the airport, and offers the limp bloom he has been examining closely.

Michael is a man of substance. Putting your arm around Michael is like hugging a bag of copra - all lumps and bumps. Michael has muscles on his muscles.

He is from Milne Bay, and his wife is from Tubeserei, where they have built a house for their retirement. Michael speaks his five languages with equal fluency and rapid-fire delivery. He will fit in well at Tubeserei; I can imagine him in his retirement conducting classes in advanced spreadsheeting or tissue culture.

We reminisce about Milne Bay, each adding names to the catalogue of our favorite places - Sideia, Esa'ala, Doini, Rogea, Kwato, Suau, Deka Deka. We comment on the repetition in "eta lau Deka Deka dekenai", but acknowledge that Motu is rarely spoken in Milne Bay today.

It's a joke in the past sense now.

***

Keith Hedu

You can't miss Keith. He is unavoidable. Keith is solid, broad, and has a very physical presence.

Born of Bena parents, Keith grew up in Goroka where his father, Auwi Miyogo, worked for Talair. Keith and his wife Rose, who is from Watabung, have four daughters - Lindsey, Cynthia, Tersher, and Roselyn. The girls are the third generation away from the daily influence of village life, and as Keith says are totally western in their ways.

We often talk about the challenges in maintaining the connection with tradition, and with traditional society. During Hamamas Week Keith is the first to tangibly support the celebration of Papua New Guinea cultural diversity by wearing his traditional Bena dress and decoration. And a handsome sight it is too.

I suggest to Keith (if it is any consolation) that all is not lost. Research in that great immigrant nation, the USA, indicates that although the first two generations turn their backs on their traditions and language and subsume themselves in the new culture, the third generation seeks to reach back to the language and values of the grandparents and re-establish its connections.

Keith is the only man in the household, and maybe this is the reason he pursues extremely physical pursuits like playing rugby. Rugby at Tabubil is not for grass field wimps. The pitch is all gravel, with which collisions are numerous and bloody. Keith shows us his grazed anatomy with the same pride as the Bena fight leaders of the past.

***

Rose Paulus

Rose Paulus is the secretary and administration officer at Ok Tedi's Environmental Centre, and the daughter of former RPNGC Sergeant Paulus Yaregawa Haunje. Rose clearly remembers, and describes, her father's participation in the long patrols out of Telefomin twenty-five years ago. She was just a young girl at the time, but vividly recalls the occasions and the patrols to the West Papua border.

Rose Paulus is Telefol, and she talks of the sense of style of the Telefol – the *pasin* (style) in Tok Pisin. Her stylish braids emphasise her point about pasin. So does her use of her own personalised, chatty greeting in her e-mail auto-reply. Rose never uses the default standard in anything she does.

Rose explains the strong traditions of the Telefol, the close community, and the expectation that people will marry locally. Rose's child carer, Jenny, is also Telefol. Jenny's mother is a custodian of her clan's traditional Telefol stories, and Jenny, carefully chosen for the task, is helping pass on the stories to the next generation.

Sergeant Paulus Yaregawa Haunje moved around regularly with his job, so young Rose also lived in Wewak and Vanimo, but returned later to Telefomin where she graduated from Telefomin High School.

After high school Rose went to Mt Hagen where she attended the Mt Hagen Technical College, graduating in 1986 as a secretary, then on to Goroka Technical College, graduating as a stenographer in 1987. She has worked for Ok Tedi Mining Limited for 15 years.

Her three children, Luey Junior, Vanessa and Tanya were all born at Tabubil.

***

Graduate Recruitment

Simply the best. Better than all the rest.

This could be the slogan for OTML's graduate recruitment program. It is not the only annual graduate recruitment program in Papua New Guinea, but it has the reputation of attracting the best people.

Certainly the best of the bright young graduates in a variety of disciplines are selected.

Invited to participate in the selection process that included having the short listed candidates spend several days on site, I am impressed by the candidates I meet - engineers, scientists, accountants, lawyers and humanities graduates. The eager; the committed. Each has high expectations, and challenges are expected as they commence their careers.

The recruitment process has a number of dimensions. The one in which I am participating is the observation of teams working on a case study. The dynamics of the team, the methods of problem solving utilised, and the interaction, will all be observed.

The team has a scenario to deal with. To give it the edge of reality it is about Papua New Guinea. Specifically it involves a mining company allocating K400,000 to a local hospital. How will the funds be put to best use? There are a number of demands for funding in the hospital - acute and emergency care, intensive care, disease prevention, research and epidemiological studies, and administration. The collective bids for funds exceed the sum being allocated.

There are six people on the team I am observing - five men and one woman.

They sit around the table. Will this be a free-for-all I wonder? As facilitator I suggest we build a simple resource allocation model and put relative values on the five categories. Hopefully this will give us a rationale for our final recommendation.

The team looks a little lost until Daniel suggests Miriam as chair. "Good idea", echo some of the others, looking at the possibilities of building alliances in the group.

Miriam takes the chair and quickly lays out the rules.

The game commences, and immediately takes on the

characteristics of improvised theatre. Jim and both Peters do not delay, presenting arguments based on the details of the case - which they all repeat. Miriam points out that we don't need to repeat the givens.

Jim looks for early compromise, but Eric is a stronger arguer, and Jim is the first casualty. Daniel also looks for the comfort of the middle ground, but Peter's response is more logical and forceful.

Miriam is chairing competently, but quietly, and starts to pursue a line. The game warms up, but cools quickly when there is an impasse. But Miriam sees an opening and quickly moves in with her compromise proposal. Her proposal is that we have to be realistic, and accept the money will not stretch beyond meeting the basics - there can be no investment in the future.

Disappointment is demonstrated in the body language. However the case study illustrates the reality of business - even big business - that resources have to be allocated rationally. It also reflects the broader reality that in Papua New Guinea the public health system does not have the resources it needs for disease prevention and longer-term studies into public health.

The excitement of the game has been overtaken by a simple reality. Lunch is a quiet affair. Some of the group looks overwhelmed – metaphorically turned away from a hospital

Assessments are made; appointments are offered.

The eager have landed.

***

Later in the day I checked the government's public health budget. The allocation of pharmaceuticals in the public health system this year divided by the population is K1 - just enough for a packet of bandages per person.

Images

(top) Tabubil. Between an ok and a hard place

(left) Karonama Ani the man I was engaged to mentor. His first loves are architecture and his family

Mary Montfort (Monty) and Adele Joseph. Monty took her first steps one Sunday afternoon in my house when in front of a crowd she engaged top gear and made a bee-line for a power point.

Serious drains for serious rains. With an annual rainfall of over eight metres, Tabubil provides opportunities for stone pitchers to display their craft.

On the steps of the "Pride of Tabubil". From the left - Rossa Ampao'i, Dorothy Petilau, Claire Omot and Delores Chow. Delores later joined Airlines PNG as a senior flight Attendant and the face of their TV advertising. The face that launched a thousand trips.

Gagl 1970. A coffee grower's meeting provides an opportunity to develop negotiation skills, and the art of the strategic withdrawal

John Waguo. John was one of the original students at Kerowagi High School. I knew John as a 15 year old with a passion for football.

Coffee census, Mondandurugl, 1969

Each day, every day, six or more semi-trailers are on the road from Tabubil to Kiunga. With over 100 wheels on the road the convoy includes a puncture repair contractor.

Chris and Judy Warrilow, Melbourne 2005. Warrilow stayed on in Papua New Guinea for thirty years after independence and worked as an adviser to a succession of Papua new Guinea governments. He was one of the Papua New Guinea government's original Ok Tedi liaison officers.

Bob and Susan Boerma
Susan was a senior executive in the corporate sector in the Philippines. Bob is from Canada. Together they created the most beautiful garden in Tabubil.

Mother and daughter flight attendants Clare and Delores Chow. Clare was Talair's Chief Flight Attendant until 1988. Delores commenced flying with Airlines PNG in 1997 and later flew with Air Niugini, National Jets, then back to Airlines PNG

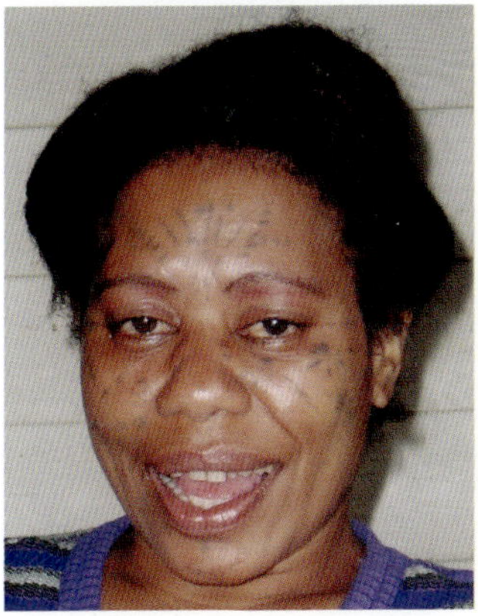

Jenny Kamai. From a village a short walk from the West Papua border, Jenny speaks the border languages of Malay (Bahasa), Tok Pisin and Awin (her mother tongue). Jenny also speaks the other official languages of Papua New Guinea - Hiri Motu and English.

With Bill Wangi, Mr. Fixit. Bill spent two years of his career on secondment to the Royal Australian Navy.

Sgt-Major Paulus Yaregawa with Luluai Melok near the Tumolbil airstrip in September 1979

Eddie Houwo is an accountant by profession. His wife is an Infant Welfare nurse and he points out the similarity in our lives.

Rose Paulus, daughter of Sgt. Major Paulus Yaregawa. There is never a default option in anything Rose Paulus does.

(left) Michael Guba was originally a horticulturalist. He brought the science of taxonomy to his later role as a materials cataloguer.

(below) Keith and Rose Hedu with their daughters Lindsey, Cynthia, Tersher, and Roselyn. Rose's farewell gift to me was a handmade ***bilum*** into which she wove the Papua New Guinea flag.

Christina Mangen works for Starwest Constructions, one of OTML's major contractors. After initially training as an actor, singer and dancer she pirouetted into the corporate world joining Starwest as senior payroll clerk.

Caroline Kereku was universally regarded as a star in the ascendancy at OTML. The light went out one night in the most tragic circumstances. The town formally mourned for a month.

Gabriel Babe undertook his master's degree in Sweden, and added Swedish and basic French to his already extensive language skills. A renaissance man in the classic sense, Gabriel's interests range from maritime law to medicine and resource economics.

Faces in the Cloud

Dr Roger Higgins' departure from Tabubil after eighteen years in PNG had considerable symbolism about it. One was the Manus dancers and drummers who farewelled him. Roger is an honorary Manus *lapan* (chief). Caroline Kangol, the Senior Flight Attendant, who coincidentally is from Manus, supervised the dancing.

Additionally, the departure was by air in a Hevilift Kingair on a direct flight to Cairns. Here was the man who arguably was the leading private sector manager in Papua New Guinea at this stage of its development.

Travelling with a subsidiary of a company that had its origins in the pioneer explorers of the 1930s - Collins and Leahy - the long-term commitment of these families to Papua New Guinea is admirably illustrated in their ongoing and diverse investment. It was fitting that a manifestation of one set of pioneers should convey such a significant latter day pioneer.

And it was fitting that Roger and Dianna Higgins chose to fly out of Papua New Guinea. Aviation is part of the vascular system of Papua New Guinea. It has been argued that without aviation Papua New Guinea as we know it today could not have existed.

It is ninety years since a plan was developed between the governments of Holland, Germany and England to explore and map the interior of the island of New Guinea by balloon. I imagine this was a project that literally did not get off the ground because of World War I, so it is almost certain that it was not until the early 1920s that aircraft were first used in

Papua New Guinea.

Australia's first military aircraft deployment was planned for late 1914 when it was agreed that aviation would have a role in identifying enemy ship locations. In the event, the two aircraft sent to Port Moresby, along with spare parts and mechanics, were never flown in PNG as the strategic situation changed.

Certainly Captain Hurley is regarded as being the father of aviation in Papua New Guinea, using two aircraft provided by the Hordern family in Sydney to conduct inaugural flights along the south Papuan coast and the Fly River.

The history of aviation in Papua New Guinea is a rich and fascinating one. It starts with the provision of logistical support for the emerging gold industry in the 1920s and 30s. Indeed history tell us that it in 1931/32 the total air freight carried in Papua New Guinea (nearly 3500 tonnes) exceeded the combined weight of airfreight carried in France and Germany during the same period. The story goes on to tell us of the support of highlands exploration later in the 1930s, chronicles the evacuation of civilians and troop movements in World War 2, and eventually comes to the commercial services that connect Papua New Guinea today. And it is so appropriate that it continues today to provide the mining industry with same logistical support it gave the gold miners three generations ago.

This history has been a recurring theme in Papua New Guinea literature, and many books have comprehensively covered the subject. But it is the scale of Jim Sinclair's three-volume work "Balus" that best reflects the extraordinary breadth of the special role of aviation in Papua New Guinea.

The defining characteristic of airports in Papua New Guinea today is not the architecture, the range of its intermodal transport connections, or the shopping experience, but the constant busyness of light aircraft movements.

Tabubil International Airport is a good example. The name may conjure up a vision of something grander, but the airport does not run to as much as a cold drink machine. The door-to-door bus from the airport to homes around Tabubil, and the car parking are free. Maybe it is the absence of outrageous charges that is the special quality that defines the Tabubil International Airport.

Tabubil is a port of entry, is serviced by direct flights from Australia, and has on-site Customs and Migration staff. Each year there are over 1400 international movements through Tabubil.

The company air charter operations are a major exercise in outsourcing. Colin Kittel, Logistics Manager at OTML, describes the charter operation as the best airline operation in Papua New Guinea in terms of aircraft quality, number of ports serviced, and standard of service. Col's background qualifies him to make such a claim – he is a pilot himself. He certainly sees Tabubil as the hub with no peer.

In any discussion on aviation in Papua New Guinea it is the names of the flyers that are usually mentioned. And they deserve all credit too. The autobiographies of Bobby Gibbes, Eileen Steenson, and Piers Courage - just as examples - are compelling accounts of their contribution.

But here are some stories of people whose contribution rarely, if ever, is acknowledged.

***

Elton Gorogo

Elton Gorogo is the aviation supervisor at OTML, and each week he is responsible for over forty company flights to domestic and international destinations. Many of the domestic charters are "milk runs", stopping at two or three destinations in a tight schedule before returning to Tabubil. There are also dozens of commercial services in and out ofTabubil each week. In addition the OTML chartered helicopter operates for about four hours a day, its distinctive baritone presence reminding us of its important role in mining operations.

Elton came into aviation supervision by chance, although the connections are logical when he explains them when sitting in the control tower at the Tabubil airport waiting on the arrival of the Sunday afternoon charter from Cairns.

He was born in Port Moresby, but spent the first sixteen years of his life on Bougainville where he was educated and learnt his family values as an expatriate Papuan. There he attended the international school to year ten, and following the family's return from Bougainville in 1989 completed years 11 and 12 in Port Moresby.

His first job was in the travel industry as a domestic and international consultant. He spent five years in this environment, learning that service is a powerful differentiator in the market. Elton brought this view of service with him to OTML and I can imagine him embracing it with even greater enthusiasm in the longer term when he sees a move into the tourist industry as likely.

Elton's appointment to OTML in 1997 as a travel co-ordinator was a logical step, and built on his travel industry experience. OTML has a large staff of Papua New Guineans and people from further a field - from all over the globe in fact. Travel is a major requirement.

After only a few months in the OTML travel role, Elton was offered the job of aviation supervisor. Elton has travelled widely in Papua New Guinea and Australia both as a travel consultant and now as an OTML executive. He appreciates that aviation is a critical component of Papua New Guinea's infrastructure, and sees a future for himself in this sector in the short term, and in the longer term after the mine closure. He peers out of the tower, turns, and comments on the tourism potential in Papua New Guinea. He adds that he thinks the opportunities in Milne Bay remain untapped, and that he must give that opportunity a shake some time. Milne Bay now has its own international airport and Cairns is only two hours away. "This could be the new Bali," he suggests.

Elton has a strong sense of family, and is a dedicated son and brother, who has taken on a carer role in the family when needed. He now has his own family. His partner, Levilla

Dickson, is from Milne Bay, and their first child, Jordan, was born in Port Moresby. Elton was present at her birth, describing it as "an amazing experience". The new life, the new daughter, has heightened Elton's optimism about the future of his country. Optimism is a key quality in people of vision.

***

"The Girls"

It's the daily OkTedi flight PX601 to Port Moresby. The two flight attendants on duty welcome the passengers in Tok Pisin, "Good morning valued customers on our flight to Port Moresby. Before take off please fasten your seatbelts and stow your tray table, and note that smoking and chewing betel nut is prohibited on the flight."

Nine flight attendants play a considerable - but often misunderstood - role in the aircraft charter operation conducted by Asia Pacific Airlines (PNG) Ltd.

"The Girls" sounds patronising doesn't it? But "the girls" are highly trained, internationally accredited, skilled members of the Ok Tedi aircrew, and no patronising is intended. The collective reference is widely, respectfully, and affectionately used.

Theirs is a first-point-of-contact-with-the-customer role, to use the modern jargon. They are the front line troops, not those who are serried two or three levels down in the organisational hierarchy.

They seat passengers, stow baggage, serve meals, give respite to mothers of fractious babies, comfort children, clean up messes, exercise diplomacy, and - when the young blades step over the mark - they will deflate egos and administer a metaphorical clip under the ear. And in the unlikely event of such a need, they will undertake the key role of supervising the evacuation of the aircraft. It is a broad role that requires upfront skills, and comfort with having to take charge. It is a public job, and not one for the retiring type of person.

They also have roles behind the scenes: organising the provisions, cleaning the aircraft, managing the office, and laundering the linen. Passengers may never see this happen, but appreciate that it occurs.

Passengers see the women on display. They see the public face of the airline. They see the people whose service quality largely will determine how the customer has felt about the travel experience. And it is a positive experience with service so intuitive I think the women are mind readers.

These women travel widely and move in international circles, but to a person refute the mythology of having a glamorous job. It is very hard work, and by night they are exhausted. Their ease in company and their international experience will help them fulfill increasingly significant roles in their country, maybe in tourism.

Each week two of the women spend Saturday night in Australia. "What are you doing on Saturday night?"

"Nothing much; just having a quiet dinner in Cairns".

The Melanesian walk in the limited space of the cabin of the Dash 8 is a glide – as graceful as an actor's. Arms move; shoulders are straight. I watch the economy of movement as these women define their space within the cabin.

The flight attendants – all women – are widely experienced in this industry, with backgrounds in Airlines of PNG and Air Niugini, and extensive travel in the Asia Pacific region. Several have lived in Port Moresby where female airline employees have been subject to systematic, energy-sapping harassment and vicious assaults. The possibility of car jacking, kidnapping and worse is a constant preoccupation. But in Tabubil the flight attendants can safely stroll the five minutes from home to the airport, and enjoy the freedom of a safe town.

Each of the women has an interesting story to tell – careers that have headed every which way – sometimes by choice; sometimes by the whims of life.

***

Margaret Dull

Margaret Dull writes poetry about the people in her life – her daughter Renagi; her father; her grandfather; her friends. There is a lot of sadness apparent in her work, which approaches the country and western genre of hurtin' songs. English is the third of Margaret's five languages, but is the preferred vehicle for her writing. Writing in more than one language, rather than writing in one and then translating the result to another, is an ability not to be underrated, and one I associate with writers like Conrad.

Like Conrad, Margaret learnt at an early age the special role and obligations of the nobility. Margaret is from one of the groups in Papua New Guinea whose land is held in matrilineal succession. Her grandfather, obviously a wise man and highly respected and loved by the family, taught her about the special obligations that come with the responsibility of allocating land. It is a responsibility Margaret takes seriously.

I ask Margaret how I spell her name. Is it "Dal" using the PNG phonetic spelling?

"No" she replies. "It's "Dull". You know; not smart," she adds in her characteristic self-deprecating way. "It's German. I have a German ancestor," she tells me in Tok Pisin, "we took his name".

Margaret has had wide experience in the tourism and hospitality sector. And "not smart" she isn't. Margaret studied civil engineering at the University of Technology in her hometown of Lae before opting for a change of career and worked for a major hotel chain until she discovered flying. Margaret has found that fluency in several languages, plus the ability to "get along" with others has been an advantage in this field.

But life is not all levity and lightness, and there is serious side to this work. Margaret has experienced the unthinkable, and had to supervise the evacuation of an aircraft after an emergency landing in the Markham Valley. She successfully completed the evacuation of the aircraft before the adrenalin ran out, and she too collapsed. She took a month to get over the experience, and spent most of the time on rest and recreation in Cairns.

Medevacs are a part of the charter operation. The reality that sometimes life may end prior to the passage of three score and ten years can be very confronting.

It was Margaret who comforted a terminally ill passenger being evacuated to Port Moresby. His illness was AIDS – obviously an illness about which people make judgments. He was used to sitting alone; his gaunt frame was used to being without company. But Margaret made her judgment too; sat in the seat the other passengers avoided, comforted him, and held his hand for the duration of his last flight. The Sisters of Charity would be proud of her.

***

Roselyn Simik

Roselyn Simik talks of growing up in Kiunga in the Western District of the Territory of Papua New Guinea, and seeing an air hostess for the first time. She vividly recalls her reaction to seeing the woman walking down the steps of the aircraft to the Kiunga airstrip and being fascinated by the uniform.

"I told my parents and teachers then that's what I want to be", Roselyn says, wearing a smile of satisfaction that would illuminate the cabin of a 747.

Twenty years later said she had earned her wings. She achieved her ambition through a passion, ability, and probably the right conjunction of the planets.

Roselyn is Western Province to the core. Her father Simik Tetra was one of the first people to live in Kiunga, and was well known in earlier days as the government clerk at a number of stations. Her mother came from across the border in West Papua a few kilometres away.

Roselyn remembers well the Australian government officials with whom her father worked, and tells second-generation stories of the first white people who visited the area.

Other than her family it was local business people in Kiunga, Warren and Joy Dutton, who had the greatest influence on the young Roselyn. They gave Roselyn her first job in hospitality, and appear as a recurring motif in her life as she describes their influence at various stages, including today. They encouraged her to explore new opportunities in commerce, manufacturing, and tourism, and always welcomed her back on the occasions when the realisation did not match the expectation.

The opportunities Roselyn explored helped her to build the skills she ultimately needed as a flight attendant. In the meantime she got to know the Fly River well and is steeped in its culture. Roselyn loves fishing and will challenge any man to be her better. When the opportunity to fly came she was working in Tabubil. Her broad background in working in offices, engineering companies, hospitality, and then as ground crew with an airline, had given her the mix of skills she needed to win that job with Asia Pacific Jets.

Roselyn Simik is the longest serving member of the cabin crew at Tabubil, and is the only woman from Western Province working with the charter company as a flight attendant.

Her languages reflect a died-in-the-wool Western Province influence. Awin is her first language. Hiri Motu, English and Tok Pisin come in equally at number two, and she can also get by in Yongom, Daru and Balimo.

Roselyn loves travel, and has made extensive visits to the eastern States of Australia. But she does not see her job as an opportunity to travel – it is just that her office is 20,000' higher off the ground than most.

She says that flying has its high points (without intending the pun), but that it is tiring work. She fears that her relative seniority conspires with her body to tell her something about the physical demands of the life. She loves the short days, and being on stand-by when no one is on leave nor likely to report in ill. Her long days start at 4.30 am and finish at 6 pm, after six hours in the air and four hours on the ground on a milk run that may take her to Hoskins, Rabaul and Madang on the one service.

She admits that she would be unable to cope with such a long day without an understanding partner who indulges her when she returns home.

How does Roselyn see the future? She is very positive about the future of her country and her province and has her own longer-term plans for life after flying. "It will be a small venture in the world of hospitality, and it will be in Kiunga" is all she will offer, flashing that smile again. I know it will be an opportunity for Roselyn to continue to leave her mark in the province she loves. And for her parents and the Duttons to continue to be proud of her.

***

Delores Chow

Delores Chow is a second-generation flight attendant. Her mother, then Clare Ling, flew with Talair (originally Territory Airlines – later Talair). She was the first Papua New Guinean flight attendant to be accredited for the De Havilland Dash 8 aircraft, and later became Talair's chief flight attendant. Delores talks with great affection of the Dennis and Della Buchanan, who founded Talair, and the Talair days. Come to think if it, so do most of us who knew the Buchanans.

Pre-programmed to the extent that she could make up her face before she had learnt to tie her shoelaces, Delores is a vision of flashing eyes and fingernails. She carries the burden of a shimmering beauty, and a smile that is straight out of the "Land of a Thousand Smiles" textbook. It can cloud the talent beneath. There is also a serious side to Delores. The job is a serious one, and Delores has an aura of authority when she takes charge. Passengers and pilots know who runs the cabin.

Delores began her flight attendant career with Airlines PNG (then MBA Airlines), graduating in 1997. She moved on to join the Pride of Tabubil in 2000.

Like her mother, Delores has several strings to her bow, and has also worked as a secretary and a hairdresser. She is up and about each flying day at 4.30 am to win the first up, best tressed award.

Flying has obvious advantages for someone who loves travel, and the names of the ports she has visited this month trip off the tongue – Honiara, Fiji, Nauru, Vanuatu, Mildura, Kangaroo Island and Devonport.

The influences in Delores' life have been largely Manus, and include her schoolteacher grandfather, her mother, her aunts and uncles and her Manus friends. Delores was born in Rabaul, and went to school in Lae and Australia. She has worked in the National Capital District and New Ireland, and is a seasoned traveller. "Do you feel at home in Australia Delores; you are there once or twice a month?"

The reply is disarmingly honest. "Not really. I feel comfortable in Australia, but home will always be home".

"And the downside of flying?"

"I don't know whether it is the hours we work, the uniform, or me, but something intimidates the men. I haven't had a date in eighteen months!"

***

Elizabeth Mathew

Liz has the ultimate backroom role; a support role that keeps the company aloft, so to speak. She manages the office, updates the technical manuals, and buys supplies.

It is curious for someone who is so energetic, extroverted, technically proficient, and creative. Liz has fitted more into 27 years than many people manage in a lifetime.

Liz was born at Tarabits, a stone's throw from the West Papua border in the remote Star Mountains. She wears mine site dress – sensible clothes and safety boots – with the Min cultural statement of close-clipped tight curls.

Liz spent most of her school life in Papua New Guinea, but was a talented student and had the opportunity to complete years 11 and 12 in Cairns. Here she won a number of awards, exhibitions and prizes, but it was also here that she discovered Gilbert and Sullivan and found she had a creative side.

Liz did not rest after completing school, but moved on to get her private pilot's license in Australia and then went to India to undertake studies in computing and become a tutor in software systems.

Australia's immigration policies allow Liz to visit regularly to work with a part-time working visa and put in some flying hours. Her only regret is that by necessity she has to fly small aircraft. The reality is that flying time in large aircraft is impossibly expensive for the holder of a private license.

Liz is a fine role model for the young people of Western Province. She has shown what can be achieved, and demonstrates the benefit of broad interests and a broad education.

Her motivation, her ability with technology, and her understanding of flying, together with a mix of the analytical and the creative, fit her well for the job she does.

It is Sunday afternoon and Liz ushers me out of the hangar for the night lock down. "Do you want a lift?" she offers. I decline, explaining that it is a balmy afternoon and I only have to wander around the corner. Liz drives off, big smile, and a wave. I could have sworn she was singing the chorus of Poor Wandering One.

All Critters Great and Small

A letter from a colleague when I was at Tabubil had caused me to think about critters.

At the time I had not thought seriously about critters at Tabubil, but for a good read about the animals of Papua New Guinea I recommended to my enquirer that his first call should be Dr Tim Flannery's Throwim Way Leg and Mammals of the South-West Pacific and Moluccan Islands.

As a zoologist, Dr Flannery beautifully captures the essence of the country. No other writer has his authority to deal with the cuddly (the marsupials), the mysterious (the bats), and the revolting (the tapeworms). Dr Flannery has the additional quality of having worked as a consultant to OTML.

But there are some critters I should mention, including three of an exaggerated scale. I was walking to work one day and saw a dead centipede about 20 centimetres long being taken apart by an army of ants and being conveyed back to a nearby nest. It was a fascinating sight.

I also saw on a footpath what looked like a piece of black umbrella fabric with parts of two ribs still attached. But on looking closer I saw that it was a butterfly. The "ribs" were camouflage, that I guess Mother Nature had provided to trick predators into thinking the critter was a large beetle.

Then there are the stick insects. One alighted on my arm in my garden. It stayed there long enough to take it inside and run a tape measure over it. It was 28 cms in length - elbow to wrist. After satisfying its curiosity it unfolded wings like a

Japanese fan and departed.

In the house there were geckoes, cockroaches and beetles. Geckoes are harmless and clean up any insects that come their way. Cockroaches are probably harmless too, although I dislike them on aesthetic grounds, and mounted a serious campaign to eradicate them. But the beetles were the most interesting. They are substantial animals that die in very public places. The ants remove their bodies after dissection. In the morning all that is usually left are the menacing mandibles that look like bolt cutters. They are too tough even for the ants to eat them.

There are snakes around the town, and sometimes flash floods in the culverts will provide an express ride to a new habitat. Extended dry spells will also upset the habitat and food source of snakes, so they range wider looking for food. I ceased walking around the garden bare-footed after a critter bit me on the ankle - it could have been a spider or a snake. Two tiny scratches about a centimetre apart led to what looked like a bad burn. Eventually the blackened skin sloughed off and it was two months before the wound healed.

But the really dangerous critters are the microscopic. Malaria is a problem out of town, as are filariasis and elephantiasis. Keep in mind that the malaria parasite and the microfilaria worms are so tiny they live in the stomach of a mosquito. One has visions of Jesuitical-type discussions about how many would fit on the head of a pin. Prevention of associated diseases is relatively easy though, and OTML won't compensate you if you get it.

Dogs

In the Star Mountains there appear to be Asiatic dogs, although the tail is less brushy. But if they are Asiatic dogs, then they are related to the Australian dingoes, and would have come to Papua New Guinea 4000 to 5000 years ago. This also means that along with the dingoes they are the animals that predate the breeding that has made today's dogs, and will eventually interbreed themselves out of existence. A sad end to proto-dog.

The Tabubil dogs do not bark, and they have the same colouring as the dingo. They are a little smaller, but have the same shape. In fact they could be confused with what today we know as the Thai dog.

The Star Mountains region is relatively isolated so they have not been bred out yet, but I know of no research being conducted.

I saw my first Asiatic dogs or "singing dogs" around the lakes of Mount Wilhelm in 1964. As the area was not as isolated as the Star Mountains there had been generations of breeding with other introduced breeds. It is likely there has been similar interbreeding between the "singing dogs" of the Lamington area of the Oro Province.

The dogs live contentedly in the urban environment of Tabubil, are friendly, seem to share the pack inclinations of other dogs, and are altogether a fairly typical example of canis familiaris.

But they yodel; they don't bark.

Snakes

Rachel relates her story in Tok Pisin, describing the garden as *naispela* (pretty). She enjoyed working in it. It is the family's main source of food, and working there reinforces her cultural heritage. She moved easily among the kaukau (sweet potato), the pumpkin vines, and the tapioca, her main tool - her bushknife - always in her hand.

She trimmed this, tidied that, and pushed in stakes where they were needed. She was proud of her efforts; happy to be working with her father - for a daughter perhaps a universal happiness that transcends cultural boundaries.

The snake she trod on defended itself with a lunge that caught her on the outside of her left foot. She screamed and pulled, but the snake had a firm grip with its fangs in the top of her foot, and used its lower jaw to maximise the purchase on the sole of her foot.

Rachel tells the group in Tok Pisin the snake gnawed or chewed. As much as she resisted, the snake held on tighter. (I am suddenly aware that I am being conned. According to my reading, no snake gnaws or chews, except the King Cobra, and it is not native to Papua New Guinea). Rachel lost consciousness in a few moments, her eyes rolled back so that only the whites were visible. She acts out the torpor; then the faint.

Within those few moments her father had killed the snake. He quickly made a tourniquet and applied it to her lower leg. He cut the wound, encouraged bleeding, and with a pipette fashioned from a piece of thin bamboo he sucked the fluid out of the wound.

Rachel said her father told her the poison was black in colour. Perhaps it was just venous blood. Maybe the devil's colour indicated the presence of venom.

Snake is highly prized as food. Those who eat it describe it as being like chicken in colour and texture, but fatter and richer. A "small" portion (indicated by her hand span - thumb to little finger) - is all one needs.

Rachel survived the bite by the snake (*kamanim* in her Telefomin language, and possibly a Papuan Black) with the assistance of a dose on antivenene from the Tabubil hospital, but her foot still carries the reminder of the attack. The envenomated site on her foot is taut, glistening and blackened rather like a burn.

Without a hint of competiveness, Annette shows us the site of a snakebite on her right leg just below the knee. She starts her story in a very matter of fact way that immediately gains attention. Annette did Expressive Arts at High School and it shows when she gets into the story, her eyes and mouth engaged as one.

Like Rachel, Annette was also in the bush, but she was making sago with her family. Sago grows in swampy country inhabited by a number of snakes - pythons, adders, and taipans. They felled a tree, and while sitting on it Annette noticed a short fat snake close to her - an adder (she uses the Faiwol word - *fiawuk*). It is a feared snake as it has a narrow white tail that conceals a needle; both ends of the snake are venomous.

It stung her with its tail - one puncture mark just below the kneecap.

She fainted from the pain, but her father applied a tourniquet and sucked out the wound as Rachel's father had done. She recovered in a few days, and the condition of the site strongly resembles that of Rachel's foot - it is black, glossy and taut.

The family killed the snake, later cooking it in hot stones and eating it. They disposed of the skeleton in the creek, but the snake's spirit, displeased, caused a landslide upstream. Annette's family had only one option. They had to recover the skeleton of the snake, burn it, and grind it into powder. They then threw the powder into the river. The snake's spirit, having nowhere to exist, disappeared and the landslide ceased.

The story is believed. Therein is its truth.

I explain that the adder does not have a sting in its tail, and that that part of the belief has no basis in fact. However to a person the group strongly defends the story. Mythology surrounding snakes is strong.

Bill adds a final note to the tale. "Only last night a snake took on a human form and came into my village to undertake a reconnoitre. He checked out the chickens and the dogs. He will be back".

Footnote. The story is as told and obviously has elements of fantasy. The snakes mentioned are venomous, but such snakes are rarely eaten in Papua New Guinea

The West Papua Diaspora

Deina

The knock at the door was very gentle – more a tapping of finger nails really. It was not an aggressive rap, but loud enough to wake me from the mid-morning sleep of recovery from the ravages of the "flu-like" illness that had struck the town.

I stirred and heard the tapping again. Awake now, I investigated.

There were three girls, one about seventeen or eighteen, the other two barely in their teens, but each "of the mournful countenance".

The eldest told me they were West Papuan refugees and that they wanted some work – perhaps in the garden.

The story was plausible. There are many refugees in the Western Province. I tested them by speaking English, which clearly they did not understand, so I took them at their word.

Deina, the eldest, explained the other two were her sisters. She was quietly animated, but the others were less confident in talking to a westerner.

Work? Well, yes, my gardener had gone home to his village in the East Sepik province and the garden could do with a tidy up. The girls were happy with a few days work weeding, tidying the garden, and cutting the grass.

They would use the money to buy food for the family. Neat and tidy, but not so they could not work in the garden, the two younger girls wore T-shirts and skirts. Deina wore a T-shirt, shorts and sandals.

It's hard for a relatively wealthy westerner to face the sadness of refugees who are just kids and ask why they had left their family in Kiunga. The reality is that there is a greater chance of work among the residents of Tabubil than any other town in the Western Province. One wonders why their circumstances are almost unknown in Australia where the news of refugees at the time had been dominated by the reports of a solitary refugee in the Manus detention centre – Aladdin Sisalem.

The reported $25,000 a day cost of his detention would go a long way among the refugees in Daru and Kiunga, and increasingly, in Tabubil.

The girls' ability in Tok Pisin notwithstanding, the next morning I greeted them with selemat pagi which was about all the Malay I can muster. They chorused their response in Malay. I didn't understand what they said, but it went some way to corroborating their story.

They put in a few days in the garden, and I was happy with the result. I saw the girls again at the market on Saturday morning. They looked well as they bought a few bags of sweet potato and greens, but there was still a sadness about them.

I did not see them at the market again, but I met them some time later in the lane running between my house and the single men's' quarters. They were wearing new clothes – basic T-shirts again, and Deina had chosen her preferred shorts. Deina turned her back to me as they stopped to allow me to pass in the narrow lane, but in response to my greeting she turned to chat and explain that she had cultivated a few friends in the single quarters. But no, she offered, she wasn't working as a prostitute.

It seemed that her interpretation of fondling for a fee was not prostitution, but I did not get involved in semantics. I never saw Deina again, but I saw her sisters some weeks later. On this occasion, it was the sisters who turned their backs to me, eyes down, as I stopped to talk.

"Deina has been hurt by her embarrassment," they said in Tok Pisin. I guessed she had gone back to Kiunga.

***

There are many refugees tapping on the doors of other countries today looking for a new life. It is easy to make judgments in the absence of all the facts.
Many countries – Australia included – rise to the challenge posed by of the plight of refugees and asylum seekers.

Australia must continue to live up to its moral responsibility in the arc of instability. It is a responsibility it cannot afford to ignore.

***

The discussion in Australia on international asylum seekers and refugees only barely touches on the emerging situation in Papua New Guinea where there are now 10,000 refugees from the Indonesian Province of West Papua. The number was a "best guess" by the Papua New Guinea Foreign Minister, Sir Rabbie Namaliu, in 2003, and I suspect it was very conservative. Estimates today go as high as 25,000. Compare that number with the few dozen who make the news in Australia.

To understand why there are West Papuan refugees - particularly political refugees - we need to look at recent history in the region.

The Dutch, controllers of the part of the world now generally known as Indonesia, assumed control of western New Guinea in the late 19th century. At the time Britain had declared a protectorate over southeast New Guinea, and

Germany had claimed the northeast of the island, along with the Bismarck Archipelago and the northwestern Solomon Islands. The effect was the partitioning of the island of New Guinea and the annexation of nearby islands.

The Dutch did little to develop West New Guinea until the 1930s, just a few years before the war that saw Japan "liberate" Indonesia. As part of this liberation, West New Guinea was occupied by the Japanese, who made a valuable contribution with the development of basic infrastructure, such as roads and airfields.

On its declaration of independence from the Dutch in 1945, Indonesia claimed West New Guinea as part of Indonesia, although the claim that West New Guinea was part of Indonesia was not universally supported. Taking a peaceful approach to its claim initially, it was not until 1961 that Indonesia threatened invasion.

In 1962 Indonesian paratroopers landed in West New Guinea, but this was more a display than an invasion. However it resulted in a UN-proposed solution that Indonesia would take over trusteeship of West New Guinea with an understanding that eventually it would be given self-determination.

Australia had concerns that for the first time in its history it now had an international land border. Australia observed developments with heightened interest, particularly as the border had only four points formally marked.

In 1962 the Menzies government sought US assistance, proposing an alternative to Indonesian trusteeship. This was unsuccessful as the Americans were pursuing other interests in the SE Asia region, and had no particular interest in Papua New Guinea or West New Guinea. Two years later Indonesia's confrontation with Malaysia (konfrantasi) over its federation plans saw Australian troops involved, and by 1965 Australian interest was stimulated further by developments in Indonesia.

Today there are many more West Papuans in Papua New Guinea than were ever expected. Certainly it was recognised there would be refugees from the Indonesian regime, as the West Papua separatist group OPM (Organisasi Papua Merdeka) was in existence in the early 1960s. The involvement of the Indonesian TNI (the Indonesian Army – Tentara Nasional Indonesia) in dealing with the OPM was expected to accelerate, and later rumours of its involvement beyond its powers in activities such as at least two murders at the West Papua copper mine site, Freeport, were not unexpected.

This is not just an issue for Papua New Guinea, but also for Australia: the international border with the Western Province of Papua New Guinea is not far away. Australia has a special responsibility in the region as a neighbour, and has a special role in supporting regional stability.

Refugees aside, there is also considerable cross-border migration from people to whom the border is a technicality splitting a clan or language group. Family connections cross the border, which many cross for purposes of family reunion, and for work. The site of the Ok Tedi mine at Mt Fubilan is only 18 kms from the Papua New Guinea/West Papua border.

The issue that relates to what I call the "West Papua diaspora" is that the border does not follow natural boundaries, although the Dutch, reflecting their characteristic wisdom, had suggested such a boundary in earlier times.

Many villages are near the international border, but until relatively recently it was unclear as to whether they were east or west of the meridian. Examples include Tarabits (near Tabubil) which is east of the border, and Oksibil and Kawentikin, which are west of the border.

One of the consequences of the developments of 1962 was a proposal by the Australian government for the establishment of a PNG-based intelligence organisation that would operate independently of, but in close collaboration with, the Australian intelligence community.

This was established in 1963 within the Department of the Administrator, with Local Intelligence Committees, and roles of local secretary, being created in three provinces. The District Commissioners coordinated the activities of this new group that largely comprised field staff of the Department of District Administration and the Special Branch of the Royal Papua New Guinea Constabulary (RPNGC).

The Western Highlands province had a particular role in monitoring Indonesian broadcasting and radio communications. Located at Gugai, near the town of Mt Hagen, a modest timber house in a field of avocado trees became the centre of Indonesian communications monitoring.

Some refugees travelled much further east, reaching Milne

Bay in 1962. In the early 1960s a number of West Papuans also attended the Port Moresby Telecommunication Technicians Training School operated by the then Department of Posts and Telegraphs, and a handful attended the Suva Medical School.

Maps brought into Papua New Guinea by refugees in the mid-60s showed the large island to the south simply called South Irian; the two islands to the east of South Irian were named South-East Irian. What were these islands? Australia and New Zealand.

What was established in 1962 became the genetic origins of Papua New Guinea's National Intelligence Organisation, and contemporary Australian Cabinet papers, released in the early to mid 1990s under the thirty year rule, were enlightening reading thirty years later.

Even more compelling however are the contemporary accounts that are more explicit than the Cabinet papers. Tony Try recounts experiences at Wutung in the West Sepik Province following the Act of Free Choice. Try describes what occurred less than a kilometre east of the international border with Papua New Guinea when the Indonesian army crossed the border into Papua New Guinea and fired on the RPNGC and Australian personnel.

If US interest was officially lacking, there was still considerable informal interest demonstrated. The US air force visited occasionally on well-wishing missions, one of the side benefits being flights to Wau for the golf, and occasional journeys further a field.

More formal interest was shown by the UK. Chief of Defence Staff, Lord Louis Mountbatten, visited Mount Hagen in February 1965. Mountbatten, accompanied by his daughter the Hon Patricia Brabourne, and the Chief Defence Scientist, Sir Solly Zuckerman, paid a visit ostensibly to open the new airport at Kagamuga. Preparations for the visit commenced in 1964, with a new sitting room and fireplace being added to the residency specifically for the comfort of CDS on his two-day visit.

District Commissioner Tom Ellis, a decorated war hero himself, greatly admired the likes of CDS, and through his network was able to court their support for the work being undertaken in the highlands.

The Dutch, through their ambassador to Australia at the time, Elink Schuurman, subtly, but surely, maintained their interest in the region. Schuurman and his wife Michelle felt quite proprietorial about "their" highlands and maintained an interest in developments on the Australian side of the border.

The first of the refugees to come to Papua New Guinea were resettled in Wewak and Mount Hagen.

Several years later in the Chimbu Province, a truck stopped outside a trade store at Kerowagi. Out stepped the eldest child of one of the refugee families we had in our earlier care. The boy we had cared for and supported in his mid teens was now a grown man, handsome and moustachioed. He stopped to embrace Pat as "his second mother".

Visiting Daru for my first time in thirty-something years,

there is a sense of déjà vu when again talking to West Papuan refugees in the Western Province. People speak of the actions of the Indonesian army in West Papua, including intimidation and the murder of tens of thousands of people. But rumour only reinforces rumour and suspicion. It is not corroboration.

However, today there are also economic refugees in addition to the political refugees. To these people, the Western province (and especially the areas that benefit from the Ok Tedi mine) is an economic paradise.

Visiting the construction of a new services facility at the Daru airport, distracted by the worker who had chosen the web of galvanised steel purlins and girts three metres above the ground as the place for a lunchtime nap, I am never the less aware of the mix of people milling around. I hope he survived his lunch break intact. Maybe the prospect of his fall was today's' entertainment for the onlookers.

Whether the people identify as West Papuans or Papua New Guineans is a technicality to many of them. People whose clan, village, or language group straddles the border (eg some of the Min languages such as Atbal and Wopkai) still find it a mystery that an artificial border has been imposed where none had existed for countless generations.

Tourism

A recurring question in any discussion on economic development in Papua New Guinea is "what about tourism?"

The potential is huge. How come there is relatively little realisation, and the country only has around 50,000 visitors a year? Compare this with the likes of Sri Lanka, Thailand and Indonesia. Here the contribution by tourism to GDP is now reported to be in double figures, and tourist jobs represent 8% of total employment.

The issues are many and complex. One simply may be that Australia, and possibly the rest of the world, just does not know where Papua New Guinea is. Two recent experiences in Australia demonstrate the poor level of understanding that Australians have of their nearest neighbour; the only country with which Australia shares an international border.

The first was in a Saturday morning broadcast on ABC radio in Canberra when the host, apparently more an expert in matters horticultural than geographical, introduced a guest from "Australia's nearest neighbour". I turned up the volume to hear the guest greet the audience in Bahasa.

The second was at the Cairns international airport when I picked up a copy of the publication Gateway to Cairns. There, in an advertisement for an international congress to be held in Cairns, was a map of the region. Papua New Guinea just was not there. It had evaporated; or maybe it had been expunged or deleted. All that were left were the letters PNG, dangling, lost, over what was probably the location of Timor. Clearly, geography did not feature in the education of the designer.

Apart from the general level of ignorance I see exhibited outside the country, I have some concerns about what I see inside the country. There appear to be several connected issues - tentativeness about the service industry generally, uncertainty about what tourism is, and an associated nervousness about the long term planning necessary for success with tourism.

I suspect that behind the tentativeness is suspicion that because tourism it is not an industry that produces a product, but rather, an industry that provides an experience, it therefore is somehow not legitimate. There are no smokestacks, holes in the ground, factories, or trees to cut down. However, activities associated with agriculture, such as forestry, and fishing, tread a path that runs parallel to tourism, and may provide bridges, especially in the areas of adventure tourism and eco-tourism.

Tourism provides customers with an experience based on the provision of a service. Despite the clear benefits in commodifying and packaging the tourist experience, the application of modern marketing approaches to its strategic management does not depend on the adoption of the noun product. Tourism clearly is not about products, and it is possible that the use of the noun product may be counter-productive, as it may give the industry the wrong focus.

A strong editorial in The National lamented the decision of a shipping cruise company to cancel a visit of the "Silver Shadow" to Papua New Guinea. Competition between countries to have cruise ships visit is intense, and significant promotion and lobbying are involved. Ongoing communication must be established and maintained with the cruise industry for it to remain enthusiastic about chosen destinations.

Several states in Australia participate at annual international cruise industry forums. The market is hungry for new destinations and the industry is constantly seeking opportunities to provide customers with new experiences. Cruises today typically will be to several destinations linked by a common theme or region. Australian destinations have recently included for the first time such places as Freycinet Peninsular, Port Arthur and Port Davey in Tasmania, thus providing luxury cruise passengers with additional diversity in their range of experiences.

But the benefits of long term planning are handsome. The economy of Victoria benefits, on average, to the tune of about $AU1 million per visit for each large cruise ship in the port of Melbourne. But a coordinated and coherent marketing strategy must be pursued in order to maintain the numbers. The Victorian government through the Department of Infrastructure established the Melbourne Cruise Ship Committee in 1996, and works closely with Tourism Victoria, the Melbourne City Council, and the broader cruise shipping industry. They speak as one at the international cruise events. Evda Marangos of the Victorian Department of Infrastructure represents Victoria at these events. She thinks long term and has a passion. Both are needed for success in this sector. Neither appears to be a quality in abundance among the leaders in Papua New Guinea.

Tourism is an industry that has long-term benefits, but also has long-term planning horizons. High levels of investment are required, but so is patience in reaping the returns. There are other characteristics: units of sale may be handsomely high, but so are costs. High levels of discipline and very strict management are needed to reach and maintain profitability.

Revenue is low during the establishment phase, so there is little opportunity for misappropriation, and driving capital equipment into the ground or conducting fire sales to generate short-term benefits cannot occur.

It is not an industry for the loner, but this in itself creates a tension. Papua New Guinea, with a population of five million, probably has only 300,000 people employed in the formal sector. The overwhelming majority of Papua New Guineans in work are employed in the informal sector. They include the self-employed, the owners of small public motor vehicles and the providers of services to larger organisations. It is not the economic climate in which tourism can be incubated, despite the obvious attractions of the country.

Herein is major issue. For tourism to be successful, it requires large-scale coordination of resources, which is at odds with the business model of the sole trader; the self-employed; the entrepreneur. But even the ultimate in the self-employed sector in tourism worldwide today, the bed and breakfast operators, have acknowledged that they must act in a coordinated way and be part of a more broadly-based experience.

Consumer behaviour in high unit of sale tourism is characterised by caution. Planning tends to be medium to long term, and there is not a lot of impulse buying. A week or ten days bird watching at Kiunga with a side trip to Tabubil is definitely high end – an Air Nuigini brochure quotes AU$7000 for the experience.

These are not overwhelming problems, or impediments to a successful industry, but rather are the issues that have to be worked through logically and methodically by long-term thinkers and committed leaders, who are rare in Papua New Guinea.

But there are positive signs. There are stirrings. There are successes apparent.

The PNG Tourism Promotion Authority is coming to terms with its mission to foster, facilitate and develop tourism development, and is developing new programs and ideas. It has a leadership role in tourism promotion, which it is keen to develop, and which the country needs.

In the wake of its pursuit of a new jingle, logo and slogan, one tunes in to the tourism opportunities in this country. The field is so fertile that slogans and jingles trip off the tongue. But ultimately the new slogan and logo of the Tourism Promotion Authority is simply "Papua New Guinea Experience".

An annual travel exposition is held in Port Moresby. This certainly helps the local industry see the "products" available, and provides opportunities to link destinations. Sir Peter Barter is the local leader in this area of endeavour. Barter with his Melanesian Explorer is now providing some of the leading travel experiences in the country. And I also notice that a cruise ship (just a small one) will be calling at Budibudi near Woodlark Island in Milne Bay. This will be a rich and enlightening experience for the visitors, and one that I hope will encourage them to speak positively of Papua New Guinea on their return home.

I am sure the people of Budibudi will connect with the visitors. The Budibudi people themselves are great sea travellers, regularly sailing across 80 kms of sea to visit trading partners to their west, exchanging a variety of their foods for a range of other foods. It is international trade in microcosm.

The visit to Budibudi seems to share the characteristics of a cruise ship visiting Port Davey in that the local economy may not get much direct benefit. However as in the Hobart/Port Davey link up, one can see how a more planned scheduling would link larger ports that have the facilities to provision ships.

In relation to the Western Province, the Business Development Group at Ok Tedi talks about the future development of the Western Province depending largely on tourism together with the two f's - fishing and forestry. It's a big vision for a big province. Let us add a third f – fingers crossed.

***

The Positive Signs are There

An early checkout from the Airways Hotel in Port Moresby coincides with the early arrival of a group of Japanese tourists. On talking to the staff who have been on duty all night and who, like the visitors, are wilting noticeably from the lack of sleep, I learn that this hotel is one of several that has targeted the

Japanese market, and has regular groups visiting. It successfully caters for small groups and provides bus tours to the popular destinations.

On a chance stopover in Port Moresby after a scheduled visit the week earlier, I am greeted by name by the reception staff at the Gateway Hotel. It was not one of those annoying greetings driven by the strange performance indicators concocted by the major international chains requiring that the customer's name be used x times during check in. Rather, it is a genuine and simple, "Hello Mr Le Fevre; you're back?"

The same occurred later that evening in the restaurant. Lydia Harry, in charge of the restaurant for the evening, also greets members of the group by name. She walks among the tables, remembering names, talking to this one and that in whatever language is appropriate - English, Motu or Tok Pisin. She happily accommodates those who want to try their limited language skills, sharing a laugh with those who are prepared to laugh at themselves, and asking us about Ok Tedi "upstairs." "Upstairs?" I enquire. Lydia explains this is what the coastal people call the highlands.

We order. In my case, it was the grilled chicken burger with chips and salad. It is a basic dish, but with some of the characteristics of a meal one learns to expect in North America, although without the obligatory whole pickled cucumber. There is a double bun, tender grilled PNG chicken, an over generous serve of chips and garden of greenery. Memorable mainly for the quantities served, the meals appeal to the miners to whom size and scale are important. What else can you expect of people who work with 4wds with a 260 tonne payload, and have a similarly sized ego?

There has to be a story here. Lydia is about the age of Madeleine, my own daughter, and they both work in the hospitality industry. I watch her uncork a wine bottle, exhibiting the same dexterity I see with Maddy, but I can never manage despite my capability at pouring and dealing with the contents.

Lydia chats to the group. She is from Kerema, and as it happens is a little older than Maddy. That is about the only difference apparent.

The people from the Gulf and Central Provinces have a cultural association that goes back hundreds of years. It is through the hiri; the formal trading of food and cooking pots that has been undertaken for hundreds of years by the people of the south Papuan coast. It is through the hiri that Hiri Motu became the trading language of the Papuan coast, and was later adopted more widely throughout Papua in the late 19th Century.

Although from Kerema, Lydia attended school in Port Moresby, which she describes as her second home. Her family now lives there. She is comfortable in either Kerema or Motu as a "first" language, and has no particular memory of learning English - it just went with her schooling.

Almost immediately on finishing High School, Lydia went into the hospitality industry where she has worked since, apart from breaks to have a family. She exhibits the pride shared by all mothers when she tells us about her daughter, Delena, aged eleven, and her son, Charlie who is five.

But she experiences pressures that are only known in a developing country with a low level of participation in the formal workforce, and no social security other than the wantok system. She has a family to support. She is the bread-winner to an extended family of three generations. She carries a responsibility that she finds almost overwhelming as so many people depend on her income – parents, brothers and children. She worries about how their needs would be met without her income.

Hospitality and a culture of sharing are qualities of Papua New Guinean people that sit comfortably within the hospitality and tourism industry.

Lydia's is a personal face to this sector of the tourist industry - the hotel sector. She represents it well.

Back at the Gateway a few months later, and stopping for poolside lunch, a young woman who is setting up for the afternoon approaches the group. She extends the hand of friendship. "Hello Mr Le Fevre; you're back?"

Public Health

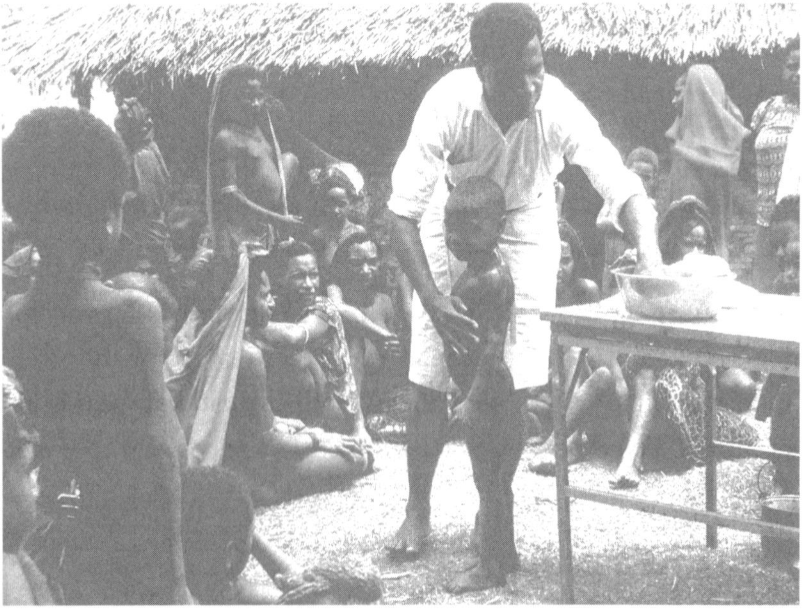

Vincent had noticed the house was occupied after its renovation and the previous family had moved into something bigger.

He also noticed the garden was in need of a tidy up, although Towns Administration had kept it tidy in its own extreme, hard-prune, way.

Vincent proposed a plan for a more delicate approach. He spoke quietly but with authority, using technical terms like pruning and composting. I asked him about his background, which included some years at a mission school where the nuns taught him the basics of horticulture. (The Christian missions have always made a huge contribution in Papua New Guinea.)

His English was good (the nuns again) but did not get much use. That we subsequently often used Tok Pisin did not help his English either.

Vincent agreed on doing a day a week in the garden. The heavy rainfall at Tabubil presents certain challenges, but he had an answer to most of them. "No, tomatoes won't grow, potatoes will rot in the ground, but tall-shouldered beans will survive if we plant them under the wide eaves," was his counsel. We agreed then on suitable local plants if we needed to add anything, although the view on which we agreed was that the trees and shrubs already there had at least proven their suitability. On reflection it was a minimalist intervention.

Vincent is from Oksapmin (widely known as Oksi) and a few months into his engagement as gardener he was called home urgently.

His father had suffered an accident.

What an understatement. Vincent's father's house had been swept away in a mudslide and crushed under a falling tree. His father had his leg broken in the process. Vincent obviously wanted to be with his father so he returned home.

The report on his return was horrific. The house, built on a high ridge, was washed away, demolished, and was now down the hill from its original location. Only the kapa (the steel roofing) survived total destruction, but was not recoverable from the valley.

His father had a broken femur, and was now in hospital pending a decision as to the treatment.

Vincent received word a few days later. His father was to be flown to a larger hospital on the coast where the leg would be amputated. The news was devastating to both of us, but this was orthopedic surgery PNG-style. Vincent left to be with his father.

My reaction was that this could not be. A result of a natural disaster, yes, but why such a final course of action? In Australia, a plate and screws would have such a condition under control in a few days and it would be likely the patient would be walking in a week. And if he had been a footballer, the leg would have been subject to attention by the best orthopedic surgeons in the land, and scrutinised by all television channels.

It exposed the reality of the chasms in the Papua New Guinea health system. It can only do so much. Scarce resources have to be rationed and used for the greatest benefit, and in any case involving major orthopedic surgery, there is always a risk of post-operative gangrene.

I had never known Vincent's father, but it took me a considerable time to accept what had happened to him.

***

The observations about public health issues that follow do not claim to be technical. I am not a medical person. But they do touch on behavioural, social, and cultural issues, and the related effect on the ordinary people.

***

It was one of those places that lends itself to clichés. Crowds milled, the heat was oppressive, and fractious children cried.

I was visiting the outpatients clinic at the Port Moresby General Hospital on a Saturday as part of a weekend break from Tabubil, I wanted to see places not visited for thirty years – the single barracks at the Public Works camp which was my first home in Papua New Guinea (still there), the house I later had (still in remarkably good condition), a friend's house around the corner (burnt down but replaced), the hospital where Pat had worked (now replaced), and the church where we were married (now a school).

The new hospital is generally on the site of the earlier Sir Walter Strong Memorial Hospital. Funded as several international aid projects – largely Japanese – the hospital includes a transport node and extensive car parking.

I had recruited a taxi driver at the Port Moresby airport for a day fee, but he explained that I would have to push start the car with him if it were to be switched off. The car's paint job was apparently by Mondrian, with panels *mumuted* (stolen or appropriated) from wrecks and left in their original colours. The driver on this occasion was a highlander so we had that in common. He dozed as I investigated. At the hospital he found a shady car park under a tree and used the opportunity for a proper sleep, reminding me that I would have to push start the car later.

The doctor on duty saw that I was showing interest in the surroundings and that I had no apparent medical reason to be there. He correctly deduced I was not there for treatment, and came over to talk to me. I told him the last time I was in the (then) Port Moresby General Hospital was in November 1963 when I was also visiting from the highlands.

I had come down for a weekend to see Pat who I was about to marry. She had in her charge a ward of young children – six months to two years at a guess – who were having facial reconstructive surgery by a team of Australian surgeons. The children were in a variety of bandages, so feeding was painstaking. I thought about their lives changing through the intervention of the surgical team, and every day since I have wondered how they are.

I was to receive nothing less that VIP attention. The duty doctor summoned up a "secretary" and two cube-shaped highland security guards who would look after me.

We walked the site. They were interested that I could still place the wards, or at least interpret the evidence in the concrete slabs and nib walls that still looked remarkably fresh and substantial fifty years after being poured.

We walked the fenced (and in some cases covered) barbed wire walkways. They reminded me of the cat races that responsible cat owners have adopted in Melbourne, but in this case it was not the native wildlife that was being protected from the cat, but the staff who needed protection from outsiders as they walk in from the carpark or the halls of residence.

I was looked after well. "Bring your wife next time," they requested.

It was a generous gesture of the hospital to treat me so well and to give me so much time. There was pride in what they did, but the limited public health budget only stretches so far, and only basic needs are met.

There are two health systems in Papua New Guinea today – the cash-strapped public, and the private, known as "international." From the accounts of my hosts, the international hospitals are expensive, and beyond the means of most. But they carry the high priced drugs the public hospitals can rarely afford, like snake anti-venene.

We walked back to the car park to find the driver stretching his legs. There were highland handshakes all round and the security guards insisted they push start their wantok's car and ensure everything was OK for our next call.

***

One of the major health issues for the PNG government is HIV/AIDS. There are concerns that the rate of infection could eventually reach the epidemic proportions of some of the African countries, where up to 25% of some populations are now infected.

The HIV virus officially was first detected in Papua New Guinea in 1987. However, thirty years earlier there were reports of an undiagnosed ailment that after the event some people are now suggesting was similar in its effect to HIV. The number of reported cases of HIV is now around 60,000, although the Papua New Guinea AIDS Council believes that five to six times this number of people could be living with the virus but are not aware of it.

The Queensland AIDS Council and the Australian Society for HIV Medicine are concerned that the unrestricted migration of Papua New Guineans across the Torres Strait provides an uncontrolled means for HIV-infected carriers to enter Australia. The PNG issue now concerns another country (arguably it always did), but there is some very reasonable Australian self-interest in the Australian government contributing substantially to education through AusAID programs.

With thousands of people already infected, and 100 new cases reportedly occurring each month, the government is talking about a pandemic. A major public awareness campaign is well under way. An issue that emerged was how explicit the campaign should be, especially in its newspaper and radio advertisements.

The tension between maximising impact and the avoidance of language that might offend was evident. But the question of what is more important seems to have been resolved, and if controlling the spread of the virus requires an affront to community sensitivies, then so be it. However, discussion on this issue continues with a clear polarision resulting.

The fundamental issue has been that the preventive means needs to be described in the common language, rather than technical, medical, or anatomical terms. Indeed, even raising the issue has led to the use of circumlocution. "We need to find the appropriate terminology to describe the sex act," the PNG medical people say. A degree of pussy footing around the subject was required to find words for the unmentionable.

From the outset I liked the Tok Pisin *koap*, but thought that I would not put money on it, for it is too explicit. *Koap* might be analogous to the f word in English or *baisé* in French - widely used and accepted, but still likely to raise eyebrows. Koap has its origins in the English "go up". It had a range of meanings in the past, but generally today it commonly refers to making the two-backed beast.

In any event the government went to considerable lengths to consult before adopting koap.

Condom was phoneticised into Tok Pisin *kondom*, and the essential message that followed has been quite explicit - if you are planning to vulcanise your relationship, then make sure your vulcanising gear is at hand.

Non-government organisations (NGOs) including Save the Children and Red Cross are helping in the battle. The report on the murder of 20-year-old Margreth Martin in Kavieng in September 2004 adds a particular poignancy. Margreth's death was not related to the Red Cross program, but it robbed the program of a committed and capable volunteer.

Foreign employees in many companies in PNG must have an HIV negative status to work in country. There are occasional embarrassments. The PNG newspapers reported that an Australian consultant investigating cultural issues related to the HIV AIDS epidemic became a victim himself when he entered into a relationship with an infected woman.

An aspect on Papua New Guinea culture in some areas – polygamy – is criticised (if not blamed) for the alarming increase in the rate of infection. Wealthy men can afford many wives and lovers, so the probability of one infected man infecting many women increases.

In areas where there is a culture of blaming women, and domestic violence is common, the consequences are predictable and stories circulate of the horrific treatment of women infected by their own husbands.

As in other countries, HIV/AIDS has become politicsed. It is reported in Papua New Guinea that malaria and betel-related cancers (oral and esophageal) have more victims, but such conditions – sad though they are – have an almost cultural position in the rhythms of life and death.

You see, HIV/ AIDS is an import.

***

The phone rings in the office. "Sorry. Can't come in today. Caught Malaria on field break".

The name malaria is reputed to have its origins in folklore. Derived from the Italian for "bad air," malaria was originally attributed to the fetid smell of a swamp. The discovery of the parasite that causes the illness did not result in a name change.

Already the scourge of tropical countries worldwide and probably killing 2.5 million people each year, its devastation will broaden with global warming. Mosquito born disease will move further north and south into new territory, or recolonise its former haunts such as northern Europe.

Malaria is almost 100% preventable and generally treatable, and OTML undertakes one of the most effective preventive interventions – vector control through the systematic spraying of the town. This has largely disappeared in Papua New Guinea towns. Although spraying is highly effective, the Papua New Guinea health budget is limited.

All OTML houses have window and door screens, long sleeves are recommended if walking out at night, and insect repellants are highly effective. OTML also provides mosquito nets for coastal people to take home on their field breaks. Is the opportunity widely taken up? No.

Preventive medication like chloroquine is also provided by the Tabubil hospital. Chloroquine is also partially effective as a treatment as it provides the relief of a quick reduction in parasite density, but will not eliminate it.

Fears that chloroquine-resistant forms of the malaria parasite are spreading in Papua New Guinea make for a gloomy story.

Largely a problem in impoverished developing countries there is little incentive for the international drug companies to invest in research. Back in Australia however, treatment is quick and effective. Doxycyclene has certain benefits as a prophylaxis and a partial cure, and research undertaken principally by the Australian Army Malaria Institute and Monash University's Victorian College of Pharmacy is directed towards a means of dealing with drug-resistant malaria.

But I suspect malaria will continue to be one of the facts

of life in Papua New Guinea until there is an oral vaccine. My observation is that it has become an excuse for a range of conditions, including the "sicky."

The Telefol

It is not politically correct to make sweeping generalisations based on the flimsiness of geography or place of birth, but I will do so. The Telefol are the people of style, of innovation, of creativity, and of education. That is a compliment, so I hope no apology is necessary. The industrious educated leave home to travel and work and repatriate the money that is the mainstay of the local economy.

Observers over many decades, expressing both affection and human compassion, showed considerable concern for the economic future of the Telefol.

One of the great explorers of Papua New Guinea, Ivan Champion, observed in his 1966 edition of "Across New Guinea," which recounted the 1928 crossing of the island of New Guinea at its widest point, "...what future have these Min people? Unless the nuclear age brings in a cheap and rapid form of transport they have no economic future."

Colin Simpson in "Plumes and Arrows" in 1962 quotes from Harry West's and Des Clifton-Bassett's reports from the late 40s and early 50s. Des Clifton-Bassett in his first patrol report observed, "...it is difficult to imagine ...the ultimate role of such a people in the Territory's economy."

Kaibelt Diria, MHA, and Assistant Ministerial Member of Parliament for Local Government, officially opened the Telefomin Local Government Council in 1968. John Ryan in "The Hot Land" quotes Kaibelt Diria asking Peter Gall, the Assistant District Officer at Telefomin "What can you do to help these people?"

Moving on, Martin Kerr in 1973 in his "New Guinea Patrol" spoke of the Telefomin people lacking in economic means to improve themselves, and Dame Meg Taylor in her television documentary "My Father, My Country" in which she retraces the walk of her father in the 1938 Black and Taylor patrol from Mount Hagen, exhibited similar concern.

Harry West, the universally admired and highly respected former government administrator, eminent District Commissioner, and United Nations adviser, was posted to Telefomin in 1950. Still travelling widely today, Harry West managed to squeeze in a letter to me at Tabubil. He recalled the times he experienced fifty years earlier, and described the extreme isolation, sparse population, and the poor soil that had led to the conclusion in the 1950s that "no economic development seemed possible."

The concern for one's fellow man was real, but the solution elusive. The list of concerned observers probably goes on.

But how the world has changed. The digital age has arrived, and Ivan Champion's nuclear age and rapid transport may have been the analogy for the developments in digital technology. Telefomin is still isolated, but less so in a world where the satellite phone services every square metre of the planet, and my e-mail address list today includes as many Telefol as any other group of people. And the people at Telefomin are talking about a tourist industry.

Rose Paulus of the OTML environment centre speaks with considerable respect about the Australian staff who served in Telefomin, removed from their families, with no Australian food, and little outside communication. I add my respect to Rose's observations. Paradoxically, the recognition of the contribution of these Australians has been a latter day development, as the Telefol who are now engaged in the development of their country and travel internationally appreciate the size of the challenges the Australians faced in earlier times.

Many talented young people move out of Telefomin to get an education. Take the three men in the Nokensengim family for example. All have bachelor's degrees from the University of Technology (Unitech) in Lae.

There is Patrick Nokensengim, with whom I worked. Patrick graduated Bachelor of Civil Engineering in 1996, and joined OTML as a graduate in 1997 under the graduate development scheme. Patrick is quiet, introspective and charming; a thinker. Atha, his wife, who graduated from the Goroka Business College in 1999 the year before they married, is a secretary at the Tabubil hospital.

Patrick works as a Civil Engineer with the Roads Section of the Engineering and Power Services Department.

Lucas Banok is Patrick's eldest brother. He graduated Bachelor of Forest Management. He has worked with the Sandaun Provincial Government, has acted as the District Administrator for the Telefomin District, but recently moved back to forest management.

If you think a pattern is emerging, you are right. There is more. Yupi Nokesengim graduated from Unitech in 1989 in Surveying and Land Studies. He is a specialist in Mine Surveying, has worked with Asia Pacific Surveys for Wafi Hidden Valley Gold Exploration, but now practices his profession in the resources sector in North Queensland.

This is a catalogue of achievement of which any parent would be proud.

It is another achievement for which OTML must take some credit.

***

Alan Bong

Telefol migration further south has commenced with a handful of engineers and surveyors now working in the Australian resources sector.

The most recent of the emigrants is Alan Bong. Papua New Guinea's loss was Australia's gain in May 2005 when Alan joined Australian Bulk Minerals in its Savage River iron ore mine operations in North West Tasmania.

Now located in Burnie, Alan and his wife Olivia and their three daughters Ruth Chloe (seven), Grace (four), and Joy (eighteen months), are enjoying the special benefits of life in a rural city. We visited Alan and Olivia in their new home in Burnie, Tasmania.

Alan is Senior Long Term Mine Planning Engineer. His work involves strategic mine planning and design, and life-of-mine studies - a significant area of responsibility.

It's an inspiring story. Alan Bong, 35 years old, is from Eliptamin. Olivia is from Telefomin, although they now consider Telefolip village to be home.

Alan was a capable student, undertaking primary schooling and some of his high schooling at Telefomin, and then completing high school at Sogeri. The alumni of Sogeri feature prominently in Papua New Guinea history, so Alan is in special company.

He then went on to University of Technology, Lae, to study engineering, graduating in Mining Engineering in 1994, and taking out the University council's medal for top student award.

His professional career includes roles with Highlands Gold Ltd as a Site Engineer in its exploration site at Frieda River near East Sepik and Sandaun provincial border, and a secondment to Porgera Gold in Enga Province.

He eventually moved to Ok Tedi Mining for two years as a Mine Planning Engineer, later as Leader Mine Production Planning, then into Technical Services, and eventually Drill and Blast. There are no damp squibs in Drill and Blast - Ok Tedi Mining Limited blows up 200,000 tonnes of mountain each day.

So now the family looks to the future and their next set of achievements, featuring among which will be the education of three new Aussie girls.

Alan has political ambitions. He has contested a seat in the Papua New Guinea parliament, but like most first-timers was not successful. I suspect that was only a minor irritation to Alan, and that we may see him pursue his interests in Australia. Tasmanian politics might benefit from some Telefol pasin (style).

***

Maria Wasinau (Kambu)

Maria Wasinau (Kambu)* relies substantially on gravity to get to work each day.

After leaving her house in Kinum Street each morning at 6.45 and pointing her wheel chair towards the White House, it is down-hill all the way. Her brother, Philip, who also lives nearby often walks with her, as does her daughter, Christine, who attends the international school at Tabubil.

If life has ups as well as downs, is there a challenge in coming home after work? Not really. Maria opts for the company car in the afternoon. She is a very practical woman and there is not much that gets in her way.

Talking to the Reverend David Aldridge, a former Baptist missionary at Telefomin and now retired and living in Burnie, Tasmania, we agree that Maria reflects the special qualities of the Telefol.

Maria Kambu is the daughter of former RPNGC Policeman Wasimnok Fangasimnok and Notromi Sitkunengim. A financial accountant with OTML, Maria was one the first Telefol to graduate in Accounting.

Although there were no favourites, Maria's graduation in 1996 was one of the proudest moments in a proud man's life. On a sunny November afternoon at the University of Technology in Lae, Wasimnok and Notromi, together with Maria's two-year old daughter Christine dressed in traditional highland attire, saw Maria graduate.

The tear in his eye and the service medals on Wasimnok Fangasimnok's jacket said it all.

Wasimnok Fangasimnok died on 31 January 2004, a satisfied, content, and happy man, whose daughters looked after him until the last. He was proud of his own achievements, but prouder of what his family had achieved. David Aldridge, fifty years after leaving Telefomin, remembers Wasimnok well, and describes him as "a fine young policeman of whom we were very fond." He shares the emotion Wasimnok expressed. It is a wonderful tribute by someone so touched by the Telefol experience half a century earlier.

Notromi today mourns the death of her husband and very close friend. "And very close friend?" I ask.

Maria makes the point that in traditional Telefol culture "and very close friend" does not always follow "husband". Notromi today is still fit, loves her gardening, climbs mountains (a necessary capability in Telefomin) and feels she is especially blessed to have five daughters who care for her. A culture-transcending quality of all daughters I daresay.

Wasimnok and Notromi Fangasimnok had six children - five girls and a boy. In a society that favoured sons over daughters, derision – even criticism – attached to the number of girls. In traditional society, Wasimnok would be seen to be wasting resources in raising and educating daughters who were expected to not complete their schooling and end up married.

It was an expectation that would not be realised.

Their first born, Sandy, was one of the first nurses to be trained at the newly established Baptist Mission School of Nursing in Telefomin. Their second born, Karen Vita, was one of the second group of female Primary School teacher graduates from the Telefomin District. Their third born, Ruth, was one of the second group of Health Extension Officers appointed to the Telefomin District and the first female Health Extension Officer in the Telefomin District.

Their fourth born was their only son, Philip. Philip joined OTML straight from High School to work in the mill laboratory, and today runs a modest poultry business in his wife's village, Wangbin, near Tabubil. Maria was the fifth born, ultimately following Philip in joining OTML.

Their youngest daughter, Rosa, is the Ticketing Officer with MAF Airlines, a subsidiary of the Missionary Aviation Fellowship, and works in Telefomin.

Years earlier, young Wasimnok, about seventeen, was seen

by the missionaries and the patrol officers to be a person of potential. They saw his ability to quickly acquire language and new ideas, and his first official job with the colonial administration was as an interpreter.

The interpreters were in a unique position of responsibility, authority, and power, in the opening up of Papua New Guinea. Language is only part of the process of communication; the cultural context adds a dimension that goes beyond the literal meaning of words, and this was where the tanimtok (interpreter) shined.

But Wasimnok Fangasimnok was not allowed to stand still. Accompanied by a close childhood friend, Pigi Kubogial, he moved on to the Boram Aid Post Orderly School in Wewak to be trained for aid post duties back at Telefomin.

However, before finishing their training, Wasimnok Fangasimnok and Pigi Kubogial were recalled to assist in the apprehension of the people responsible for the killing of four patrol officers and police officers in 1953.

This was a tragic low point in the history of the colonial administration and has been the subject of many accounts in recent literature.

Wasimnok Fangasimnok and Pigi Kubogial again had to pack their bags, this time for a move to Goroka to train as police. They were in the second Telefol intake.

Wasimnok Fangasimnok's first posting in his new role was to Vanimo. His subsequent postings included Mt Hagen,

Tabibuga and Koinambe in the Western Highlands, Porgera and Wapenamanda in Enga, Ukarumpa and Kainantu in the Eastern Highlands and Lae in Morobe. Whilst on his second posting to Telefomin, he patrolled as far as the West Papuan border, the Southern Highlands border with the West Sepik, and the North Fly. Wasimnok Fangasimnok's final posting was Telefomin. He retired from the RPNGC on 1 June 1988, and ran a trade store until he died at home on 31 January 2004.

In 1955 Wasimnok Fangasimnok married Notromi Sitkunengim. Photos taken at about that time by the Reverend David Aldridge show a handsome young man and a young Telefomin village girl, looking a little cold despite the sun in her eyes.

It was while on posting to Porgera in 1972 that Maria then aged three, contracted poliomyelitis, resulting in paraplegia. Understandably this has resulted in a number of challenges in Maria's life, but they are challenges she has met head on and dealt with.

OTML has allocated Maria a spacious ground floor house that provides the access, space, and general wheel-chair friendliness needed. She has had a housekeeper in the past, but today chooses to share her house only with her daughter, Christine. Born in Tabubil in 1994, Christine attends the Tabubil International School. Between them they manage life independently, but Maria acknowledges OTML's support. I am not surprised when she tells me "Ok Tedi is good and really takes good care of us."

Looking back, Maria attributes her ability to cope with being brought up not recognising she had a disability. She was just one of the girls, and had her set chores. Her neighbours, brother and sisters also treated her no differently, so the expectation Maria learnt was that she is no different.

Then there is the challenge of bringing up a daughter and keeping her connected to her dual Telefol and Chimbu cultures, and the associated complication of "which language we should use?" So it's English at work and school, Tok Pisin at home, and the sweetness of an emerging ability in the Telefol Min language that young Christine is acquiring on her visits to Telefomin.

Maria initially graduated with a Diploma in Accounting in 1992, and commenced work with OTML as an accounts payable clerk early in 1993. After her graduation with a bachelor's degree in 1996, she soon became a Financial Accountant with the company.

Maria is strongly committed to community service, and her latest project brings together her professional credentials and her strong Telefol connections. Maria is helping the women of Telefomin prepare for their National Apprentice Trade Testing Board (NATTB) examinations for office administration apprenticeships.

She is conducting basic accounting classes for them.

Beyond that her ambitions include studying for and obtaining a Master's Degree in Australia.

Just as Wasimnok experienced in his career, Maria is not going to stand still.

- Maria is in the process of adopting her maiden name

The Last Katamano (Farewell)*

There are always mixed feelings when moving on. There is an inclination to want to remember the good and ignore the not so good, although in this case all the experiences were positive.

The opportunity to work in the Star Mountains had particular significance, as I had wanted to visit that part of Papua New Guinea since 1963. This was the year a major exploration of the Star Mountains was to be undertaken by the British Museum, and for which I was one of the liaison officers, not that I undertook much liaison.

"That was forty years ago" I hear myself say. "What will happen over the next forty years?"

As the population of Papua New Guinea increases to ten million in that time will the old issues still fester, or will new challenges emerge and supersede them? Will the Papuan people who today are rightly aggrieved at losing their Australian citizenship through an act of parliament in 1975 still be aggrieved? Will the Gena and Siklu land dispute at Kerowagi continue?

Over that same forty years the PNG Sustainable Development Program Limited will invest in infrastructure in the Western Province. I wish it the best of luck and success.

***

So much of Papua New Guinea remained unchanged after a long absence, but major changes had obviously occurred. There was the unchanged friendliness of the people, but so many were now the graduates, the leaders of industry, the scientists, the engineers, the doctors and the leaders. The natural beauty is still a major attraction, but indiscriminate forest logging is creating its own set of problems. A similar set of circumstances surrounds the West Papuan situation today as I had experienced with refugees in the 1960s.

My reaction to OTML had been totally positive despite the residual public image problem with which it has had to deal. This may be changing as OTML moves into its next phase, but the stock criticisms recur.

I was proud to have been part of the OTML story, and proud to have been part of the multi-national team that worked with the Papua New Guineans who so clearly showed their capability. It was a pleasure working with them.

The town of Tabubil, with the same sense of community and mutual support that characterised the towns of an earlier time has none of the problems generally associated with Papua New Guinea today. It has all the services associated with a small country town in Australia and the same palpable friendliness.

I made many friends and inevitably a big send off was proposed. I requested this did not happen, but a sumptuous lunch was provided instead on the eve of my departure. Naturally, the no-alcohol-on-site rule was observed. Just as well too as many of my colleagues were emotional enough as it was.

I had also requested no farewell at the airport; the flight to Cairns departs at daybreak and the people already work a long day.

Later in the evening I called on several friends and neighbours to whom I had become variously friend, father, or grandfather. I dropped off some presents here and there and collected a few too. One was a traditional bag for Madeleine – a bilum. To the Telefol a bilum is a gift and not a traded item, but the gift carries with it reciprocal obligations of friendship.

Reciprocal obligations of friendship. How appropriate I thought.

Dinner afterwards was a quiet affair with a small group of consultants. On the way home I heard a voice from the shadows call "Goodnight *Papu* (Grandpa in Manus). *Lukim yu* (see you). Send me some pencils". It was Elijah, one of my little neighbours.

***

The flight attendants on duty on the flight out were Caroline Kangol and Davina Marc, from Manus and Suau respectively. However they both said goodbye in the local language, using the Faiwol farewell – "katamono Laurie." I left the aircraft in Cairns with polite hand shakes all round.

But was it all over? No. I have regular, and increasing, contact with my former colleagues on site. It can be an e-mail asking about a clause to include in a contract, or my suggestion for a source of a product or service. It can be a Papua New Guinean family coming through Melbourne on their way to take up a job in the resources sector in Western Australia, and looking for the chance for a coffee between flights. It can be an OTML executive attending a conference, or a colleague making regular visits to Melbourne where his wife and son live while she finishes her business degree. It can be an old friend seeking help in writing a resume or seeking a reference. It can be a Government Minister or an official of the Parliament just catching up.

And the best of all is when the phone rings and I sense the delay with the satellite link so guess it is either Papua New Guinea or an off-shore telemarketer, and out of the silence comes Karonama's voice saying "Hey *tura* (friend in Motu). What's happening?"

It is not all over.

It just a new beginning.

**Katamono*, and variations such as the Telefomin *katamono* means farewell, goodbye, adieu, and seeya in some of the Min languages.

ACKNOWLEDGEMENTS

The kind assistance of the following people is acknowledged–

The Reverend David Aldridge, former Baptist missionary in Telefomin in the 1950s, for access to his photographs of the period

Mr Tony Friend, former kiap and friend of the Telefol, for his photographs

Mr Greg Holden, for access to his Kerowagi High school magazines

Ms Evda Marangos, Station Pier/Cruise Shipping Manager, Department of Infrastructure, Melbourne, for discussions on the cruise shipping industry

Ms Clare Chow, Ms Delores Chow, Ms Jenny Kamai, Ms Christine Mangen, and Ms Angela Milali for their photographs

Mt Tony Try, for his first hand accounts of life on the border in the 1960s

Mr Yanzan Tonny Aki, of the OTML Community Relations Department, for his encouragement to include stories of the old days for the benefit of his children

Dr Roger Higgins, former Managing Director of OTML, for his support for the initial idea

Mr Keith Faulkner, Managing Director of OTML, for his permission to use OTML photographs

And finally, the good people of Tabubil who assisted, patiently told their stories, shared food and drink, and often "had a lend of me" in the interests of improving a good story.

ABOUT THE AUTHOR

Laurie Le Fevre lived and worked In Papua New Guinea from 1961 to 1971, and later returned to work there in 2001.

His interest and involvement in Papua New Guinea matters continued through the intervening period. A strong connection was maintained through several Australia/Papua New Guinea cultural and friendship networks, hosting Australian visits by Papua New Guineans, holidaying in Papua New Guinea, and his roles in several Australian government agencies.

In 2000 he received an award from the government of Papua New Guinea in recognition of services to the development of the country.

Order your copy of:

CLOUDLANDS MEMOIRS

			Qty
ISBN 1 920785 74 4	RRP	AU$29.95	.....
	Postage within Aust.	AU$ 9.00	.....
		________	
	TOTAL*	$________	

*All prices include GST

Name:______________________________

Address:______________________________

____

____

Phone:______________________________

Email address:______________________________

Method of Payment:

Money Order ❑ Cheque ❑ American Express ❑ Mastercard ❑ Visa ❑

Cardholders Name:______________________________

Credit Card Number:______________________________

Signature:____________________Expiry Date:__________

Allows 21 days for delivery.

Payment to:

Better Bookshop (ABN 12 067 257 390)
PO BOX 12544
A'Beckett Street, Melbourne,8006
Victoria, Australia
Fax: +61 3 9662 2622
Email: betterbookshop@brolgapublishing.com.au